Islamic Law: A Very Short Introduction

VERY SHORT INTRODUCTIONS are for anyone wanting a stimulating and accessible way into a new subject. They are written by experts, and have been translated into more than 45 different languages.

The series began in 1995, and now covers a wide variety of topics in every discipline. The VSI library currently contains over 650 volumes—a Very Short Introduction to everything from Psychology and Philosophy of Science to American History and Relativity—and continues to grow in every subject area.

Very Short Introductions available now:

ABOLITIONISM Richard S. Newman
THE ABRAHAMIC RELIGIONS
  Charles L. Cohen
ACCOUNTING Christopher Nobes
ADAM SMITH Christopher J. Berry
ADOLESCENCE Peter K. Smith
ADVERTISING Winston Fletcher
AERIAL WARFARE Frank Ledwidge
AESTHETICS Bence Nanay
AFRICAN AMERICAN RELIGION
  Eddie S. Glaude Jr
AFRICAN HISTORY John Parker and
  Richard Rathbone
AFRICAN POLITICS Ian Taylor
AFRICAN RELIGIONS
  Jacob K. Olupona
AGEING Nancy A. Pachana
AGNOSTICISM Robin Le Poidevin
AGRICULTURE Paul Brassley and
  Richard Soffe
ALBERT CAMUS Oliver Gloag
ALEXANDER THE GREAT
  Hugh Bowden
ALGEBRA Peter M. Higgins
AMERICAN BUSINESS HISTORY
  Walter A. Friedman
AMERICAN CULTURAL HISTORY
  Eric Avila
AMERICAN FOREIGN RELATIONS
  Andrew Preston
AMERICAN HISTORY Paul S. Boyer
AMERICAN IMMIGRATION
  David A. Gerber
AMERICAN LEGAL HISTORY
  G. Edward White

AMERICAN MILITARY HISTORY
  Joseph T. Glatthaar
AMERICAN NAVAL HISTORY
  Craig L. Symonds
AMERICAN POLITICAL HISTORY
  Donald Critchlow
AMERICAN POLITICAL PARTIES
  AND ELECTIONS L. Sandy Maisel
AMERICAN POLITICS
  Richard M. Valelly
THE AMERICAN PRESIDENCY
  Charles O. Jones
THE AMERICAN REVOLUTION
  Robert J. Allison
AMERICAN SLAVERY
  Heather Andrea Williams
THE AMERICAN WEST Stephen Aron
AMERICAN WOMEN'S HISTORY
  Susan Ware
ANAESTHESIA Aidan O'Donnell
ANALYTIC PHILOSOPHY
  Michael Beaney
ANARCHISM Colin Ward
ANCIENT ASSYRIA Karen Radner
ANCIENT EGYPT Ian Shaw
ANCIENT EGYPTIAN ART AND
  ARCHITECTURE Christina Riggs
ANCIENT GREECE Paul Cartledge
THE ANCIENT NEAR EAST
  Amanda H. Podany
ANCIENT PHILOSOPHY Julia Annas
ANCIENT WARFARE Harry Sidebottom
ANGELS David Albert Jones
ANGLICANISM Mark Chapman
THE ANGLO-SAXON AGE John Blair

Available soon:

For more information visit our website

www.oup.com/vsi/

Mashood A. Baderin

ISLAMIC LAW

A Very Short Introduction

OXFORD
UNIVERSITY PRESS

OXFORD
UNIVERSITY PRESS

Great Clarendon Street, Oxford, OX2 6DP,
United Kingdom

Oxford University Press is a department of the University of Oxford.
It furthers the University's objective of excellence in research, scholarship,
and education by publishing worldwide. Oxford is a registered trade mark of
Oxford University Press in the UK and in certain other countries

Published in the United States of America by Oxford University Press
198 Madison Avenue, New York, NY 10016, United States of America

British Library Cataloguing in Publication Data
Data available

Library of Congress Control Number: 2020942292

ISBN 978-0-19-966559-4

Printed in Great Britain by
Ashford Colour Press Ltd, Gosport, Hampshire

Contents

Preface

Islamic law is one of the major legal systems in the world today. It is applied diversely as part of state law in most Muslim-majority states of the Middle East, Asia, and Africa. It also has strong influence among Muslim communities living in the West and Muslim-minority states globally. Yet, it is probably the most misunderstood legal system today, especially in the West.

From the beginning of the 21st century, troubling incidents in different parts of the world, contentiously ascribed to Islam, have led to increased global curiosity about Islamic law. Consequently, more academic institutions in the West now have different Islamic law modules on offer. This title on Islamic Law in the OUP VSI series is, therefore, long overdue and I am honoured to be its author. The content is based partly on the Islamic law module I have taught for the past thirteen years in the law department of the School of Oriental and African Studies (SOAS), University of London. Islamic law has been taught at SOAS University of London since 1948 and it remains an acknowledged centre of expertise on Islamic law globally. The analyses herein benefit from probing questions on both classical and contemporary perceptions of Islamic law that I have encountered from students over the years.

This text provides a concise understanding of Islamic law by analysing its development, theories, substantive scope, and practice. In balancing brevity, breadth, and depth, the text has been more difficult to write than I initially envisaged. It covers not merely the basics of Islamic law but also engages critically with necessary theoretical and practical points, making it a concise but probing introductory text. It offers an analysis of Islamic law based on both classical and contemporary scholarly perspectives on the subject.

Throughout the text, reference to Qur'anic verses is indicated by the letter 'Q' followed by the chapter and verse numbers separated with a colon mark. Thus, Q96:1 refers to Qur'an chapter 96 verse 1. Quotations from *hadīth* compilations are followed by the source in brackets. Also, the abbreviation 'pbuh', acronym for 'peace be upon him', appears in brackets only once after the first occurrence of Prophet Muhammad's name in Chapter 1, but should be deemed repeated after the Prophet's name throughout the book.

Mashood A. Baderin, Ph.D.
Professor of Laws
SOAS, University of London.
March 2020.

List of illustrations

Chapter 1
Historical development

The history of Islamic law is linked with the divine call of Muhammad (pbuh) to prophethood and the consequent emergence of Islam as a religious faith in Arabia in the 7th century. Muhammad was born in Makkah in then Arabia around 569 CE. At the age of 40, around 609 CE, Muslims believe that he started receiving divine revelation from *Allah* (God) through visitations of Angel *Jibrīl* (Gabriel). The first visitation was in the cave of *Hirā'* on a mountain at the outskirts of Makkah where Muhammad occasionally observed spiritual seclusion to reflect about the social malaise in his society then (see Figure 1). The verses in Q96:1–5 are acknowledged by Muslims as the first Qur'anic revelation from God to Muhammad, which marked his appointment as a prophet and messenger of God to humanity (see Figure 2). This was followed by subsequent periodic visitations by Angel Gabriel with piecemeal revelations of other verses of the Qur'an to Prophet Muhammad for a period of approximately twenty-three years until his death in 632 CE. Theologically, Muslims believe that Prophet Muhammad is the last of a long list of prophets, starting with Adam and including Abraham, Noah, Moses, and Jesus, who were all sent by God with revealed scriptures to guide mankind. Muslims also believe that the Qur'an is the final revelation of God to humanity. Muhammad's prophethood is asserted in Qur'anic verses such Q36:2–3—'By the

Qur'an, full of wisdom. You [Muhammad] are indeed one of the messengers [of God].'

Initially, the Qur'an served only as religious admonition for the early Muslims, but soon became the main source of reference for guidance in all their affairs. Thus, faith in God as the divine authority, in Muhammad as a prophet of God, and in the Qur'an as a divine revelation, has served as the cornerstone of Islamic law from the 7th century up to the present day. In *Islam: A Short History*, Karen Armstrong rationalizes this by noting that 'Muhammad had perceived the great problems confronting his people at a deeper level', which led him to 'delve deeply and painfully into his inner being' seeking a solution that was both socio-politically viable and spiritually illuminating, the answers to which came in the form of Qur'anic revelations from God.

The historical development of Islamic law may be roughly divided into six major periods, namely: (i) the formative period,

1. Muslim pilgrims visiting the cave of *Hirā* at the outskirts of Makkah, where Prophet Muhammad is believed to have received the first revelations of the Holy Qur'an in the year 609 CE.

2. A calligraphic writing of Q96:1–5—The first revealed verses of the Qur'an received by Prophet Muhammad in the year 609 CE.

(ii) the pre-classical period, (iii) the classical period, (iv) the post-classical period, (v) the modern period, and (vi) an emerging post-modern period.

The formative period

Muslim scholarship identifies the era of Prophet Muhammad as the formative period of Islamic law. It covers a period of about twenty-three years, from his call to prophethood in 609 CE up to his death in 632 CE. This consists, approximately, of thirteen years spent in his city of birth, Makkah, and ten years spent in Madīnah where he and his followers had migrated in 622 CE due to the religious persecutions they faced in Makkah.

The Qur'anic verses revealed in Makkah centred mostly on faith-building, monotheism, warning about the end of time, life hereafter, good behaviour, and religious devotion generally. Conversely, the revelations in Madīnah, while still calling to faith, provided rules on social organization in response to the needs of the established and growing Islamic polity. Apart from the Qur'anic revelations, the early Muslims also paid attention to the Prophet's personal statements and actions, which formed the foundation of his *Sunnah* later reported in *ahādīth* (sing. *hadīth*) and followed by early and latter Muslims in addition to the Qur'an.

3

The early Muslims looked to Prophet Muhammad for guidance on both spiritual and temporal matters. He provided answers to their enquiries in one of three ways: (i) by reference to existing Qur'anic verses; (ii) through revelation of new Qur'anic verses; or (iii) through his own inspired statements. The Qu'ran contains many verses that were revealed in response to specific questions posed to the Prophet by his companions. For example, Q2:219—'They ask you about wine and gambling; say: "In them is great sin, and some benefit for people, but the sin in them is greater than the benefit in them"; and they ask you about what they should spend; say: "the affordable"; thus does God make clear to you His signs for you to reflect on.' Other examples of revelations in response to specific questions or incidents are Q2:189; 2:215; 2:217; 2:220; 2:222; 3:4; 8:1; 17:85; and 20:106, amongst others. There are also many reported *ahādīth* of the Prophet in which he responded to enquiries with his own inspired statements as guidance. For example, one *hadīth* states that a man came to the Prophet to ask for general counsel, to which the Prophet responded: 'Do not get angry' repeating it several times (al-Bukhārī). Muslims acknowledge this as general guidance from the Prophet enjoining them to control their anger.

The revelation of the Qur'an was completed during the Prophet's lifetime and was fully committed to memory by himself and many of his companions such as 'Uthmān ibn Affān and 'Abdullah ibn Mas'ūd. There was no official written compilation of the Qur'an during the Prophet's lifetime, but some of his companions had private manuscripts of fragments of the Qur'an written on parchments and other materials. In 2015, two pages of ancient Qur'anic manuscripts estimated to have been written on parchment dating back to between the late 6th and mid-7th centuries were discovered in the University of Birmingham Mingana Collection of Middle Eastern manuscripts held in the Cadbury Research Library and ascertained as one of the oldest known Qur'anic manuscripts in the world today (see Figure 3).

3. The manuscript of parts of the Qur'an discovered at the University of Birmingham in 2015 written on parchment dating between 568 CE and 645 CE.

Similar to the Qur'an, many of the Prophet's companions, such as 'Abd al-Rahmān ibn Sakhr, popularly known as Abū Hurayrah, and the Prophet's wife, 'Ā'ishah bint Abī Bakr, had personal notes of his traditions which they preserved as private manuscripts. The companions who had preserved the Prophet's traditions during his lifetime subsequently became leading and trusted reporters of the Prophet's *ahādīth* after him.

Classical Muslim scholarship asserts that the Qur'an and the Prophet's *Sunnah* were established as the two main sources of Islamic law during this formative period. This is usually illustrated by reference to a *hadīth* in which the Prophet had asked one of his companions, Mu'ādh ibn Jabal, whom he had delegated to Yemen, what would he rely on in deciding cases there. Mu'ādh replied: 'I will judge with what is in the book of God [the Qur'an].' The Prophet then asked: 'And if you do not find a clue in the book of God?' Mu'ādh answered: 'Then with the *Sunnah* of the Messenger of God.' The Prophet further asked: 'And if you do not find a clue in that?' Muʿādh replied: 'I will exercise my own reasoning' (*ajtahid raʾīy*). The Prophet was pleased with the answers provided by Muʿādh (Abū Dāwud). Thus, not only were the Qurʾan and the *Sunnah* established as the main sources of Islamic law during the era of the Prophet, the possible use of *ijtihād* (independent juristic reasoning) was also acknowledged through the answers provided by Muʿādh.

Also, of legal significance in this period is a document adopted by the Prophet on his arrival in Madīnah setting out the relationship between the Muslims, Jews, Christians, and other local tribes of Madīnah. This document is known in Islamic legal history as 'wathīqah al-Madīnah' (the Charter of Madīnah) and is often described by Muslim legal historians as the first written constitution in the world. Shelomo Goitein noted that the content of the charter 'betrays a highly legalistic and even formalistic mind', and Zafar Ansari described it as throwing 'light on the Prophet's capacity to devise a socio-political structure which is conducive to the realization of the objectives' of his mission. Through that charter, the Prophet set a precedent for the recognition of secondary legislation in the form of treaties and statutes, which were also to be binding under Islamic law pursuant to Q5:1—'O you believers, fulfil [all] covenants.'

The perception of the Prophet's era as the formative period of Islamic law has been contested in Western scholarship, starting with the writings of Ignaz Goldziher from the late 19th century. Joseph Schacht escalated this contestation with particular reference to the establishment of the *Sunnah* as a source of Islamic law. They postulated that Prophet Muhammad and his immediate successors were only concerned with Islamic religious norms and not Islamic legal development as such. Those contentions have been rebuffed by other leading scholars of Islamic legal history such as Shelomo Goitein, Harald Motzki, and Wael Hallaq. In Goitein's view, it is clear from the context of the

Qur'an that Prophet Muhammad had envisaged law as part of the divine revelation he was receiving right from the beginning. Motzki also noted that 'already in the first/seventh century, people consciously resorted to the Qur'an and to rulings of the Prophet as sources of the law, if not as extensively as in later times'. Similarly, Hallaq concluded that the foundation of Islamic law was laid by the Qur'an from the period Prophet Muhammad began to receive the revelation.

Weighing the different classical and contemporary scholarly analyses, it is reasonable to conclude that, although a standardized system of law was not yet established at the time, the Prophet's era qualifies as the formative period when the foundation of Islamic law was laid with the Qur'an and the *Sunnah* as its main sources. The succeeding generations of Muslim rulers and jurists later built the formal structures for the development of Islamic law into a concrete legal system upon this foundation.

The pre-classical period

The death of Prophet Muhammad ended the period of revelation and ushered in the era of his most significant companions, the four successors (caliphs) who led the Muslim polity consecutively in the first twenty-nine years after his death. They were Abū Bakr al-Siddīq who ruled from 632 to 634 CE, 'Umar ibn al-Khattāb from 634 to 644 CE, 'Uthmān ibn Affān from 644 to 656 CE, and 'Alī ibn Abī Tālib from 656 to 661 CE, together known as the 'rightly guided' or the 'orthodox' caliphs (*al-khulafā' al-rāshidūn*). Their era is categorized as the pre-classical period of Islamic law in which the foundation laid in the Prophet's era was further developed.

It began with Abū Bakr al-Siddīq as the first caliph from 632 CE and lasted until the death of the fourth caliph, 'Alī ibn Abī Tālib, in 661 CE. During this period, Muslims continued to rely primarily on the Qur'an and the Prophet's *Sunnah* as the main sources of

Islamic law. In resolving issues, the orthodox caliphs applied relevant Qur'anic provisions, and in cases where no specific Qur'anic provision was found, they enquired whether there was any known precedent of the Prophet's *Sunnah* on the matter. There are many recorded examples of following the Prophet's precedents during the reign of each of the four caliphs. They also exercised executive political discretion (*siyāsah*) in the best interest of the community, whenever necessary.

The official written compilation of the Qur'an was completed during this period to preserve it and ensure a single textual authority, consequent to the death of many Qur'an memorizers in battle around 632 CE. The first official compilation was undertaken by a committee constituted by Caliph Abū Bakr around 633 CE. However, some private manuscripts remained in circulation then, which led the third caliph, 'Uthmān, to appoint another committee, during his reign, to verify the first compilation and adopt a single unified text. This led to the adoption of the official Qur'anic 'vulgate' known as the 'Uthmānic compilation around 653 CE. Consequently, all private manuscripts were destroyed and copies of this official compilation were sent to the main provinces of the Islamic empire at the time. The 'Uthmānic compilation is acknowledged by Muslims globally as the complete Qur'an revealed to Prophet Muhammad and passed down through generations to the present day. Copies of the original 'Uthmānic compilation of the Qur'an are preserved today in the Hast Imam Library in Tashkent, Uzbekistan and in the Topkapi Palace Library in Istanbul, Turkey (see Figure 4).

Hallaq has noted that the official compilation of the Qur'an 'must have had a primary legal significance, for it defined the subject matter of the text and thus gave the legally minded a *textus receptus* on which to draw'. The official compilation of the Qur'an was an exercise of executive discretion based on *ijtihād* by Caliph Abū Bakr and Caliph 'Uthmān, respectively, for the purpose of preserving the Qur'an for posterity, after necessary consultation

4. Copies of the original manuscripts of the 'Uthmānic compilation of the Qur'an preserved in the Hast Imam Library in Tashkent, Uzbekistan and in the Topkapi Palace in Istanbul, Turkey.

with other companions in conformity with Q42:38—'...and their affair is by consultation amongst themselves'.

There are also recorded examples of the use of *ijtihād* by each of the other orthodox caliphs during this era. For example, Caliph 'Umar suspended applying the punishment for theft prescribed in Q5:38 at a time of famine during his reign. Also, Caliph 'Alī is recorded to have exercised *ijtihād* on the inheritance question about a deceased survived by a wife, two daughters, a father, and a mother. The fixed Qur'anic shares for these heirs are ⅛, ⅔, ⅙, and ⅙, respectively, which sums up to 1⅛, exceeding a whole number and, thereby, in excess of the estate. He proposed a proportional reduction of the respective Qur'anic shares, creating, for such cases, what is referred to as the *'awl* (increase) or *minbariyyah* (pulpit) doctrine, which will be explained in Chapter 7.

During this period, Islamic rule expanded beyond the Arabian Peninsula to places like Syria, Egypt, Iraq, and Persia, and Islamic law grew with that expansion. Administratively, the Islamic empire was organized into provinces with governors and judges delegated for the application of Islamic law in the different provinces, while the central seat of governance remained in Madīnah. The practice of *ijtihād* was consolidated during this period due to emergence of novel cases that had no specific precedent from the Prophet's era and for which the companions had to find answers. They exercised *ijtihād* within the context of the Qur'an and *Sunnah* in those instances, in consonance with the *hadīth* of Muʿādh earlier mentioned in the Prophet's era. Thus, the concept of *ijtihād al-sahābah* (juristic reasoning of the companions) evolved in this era. Also, relevant customs of the new territories that were not violative of the Qur'an and the *Sunnah* were accommodated as part of Islamic law, based on the principle of legality (*ibāhah*).

Although, the Prophet's *Sunnah* served as the second source of reference during this period, there was no official written compilation of *ahādīth* undertaken at the time. Reliance, in respect of the Prophet's *Sunnah*, was on oral reports or private records and corroborations by relevant companions of the Prophet who had heard and memorized or privately recorded particular traditions. One of the companions who is reported to have held private records of the Prophet's traditions was ʿAbdullah ibn ʿAmr ibn al-ʿĀs. This era of Islamic law ended with the death of the fourth orthodox caliph, ʿAlī ibn Abī Tālib, in 661 CE.

The classical period

The classical era of Islamic law covers a period of about 600 years of dynastic rule, consisting of Umayyad rule from 661 to 750 CE and Abbāsid rule from 750 to 1258 CE. Despite different political shortcomings in this era of two dynasties, it was a period of legal consolidation and transformation during which Islamic law and its administration witnessed significant evolution in response to different realities and challenges over the long period. The period encompasses the so-called 'golden age' of Islamic civilization.

The Umayyads came to power after a civil war that led to the assassination of the fourth caliph, ʿAlī ibn Abī Ṭālib, and the formal emergence of the *Shīʿah* faction in Islam, a schism that had begun earlier as a protest by supporters of ʿAlī ibn Abī Ṭālib against the appointment of Caliph Abū Bakr as the Prophet's successor. Under Ummayad rule, the central seat of government was moved from Madīnah to Damascus. The move had significant impact on the development of Islamic law due to the different circumstances prevailing in the new capital. Under the Umayyads, Islamic territory expanded further into North Africa, Central Asia, the Middle East, and parts of Europe such as Spain and Greece, bringing more people of different cultures into Islam and under Islamic rule. The period witnessed different political, cultural, religious, and secular challenges, which Islamic law responded to pragmatically within the context of the divine sources.

The sectarianism of this period led to the spread of fabricated traditions falsely attributed to the Prophet by different groups to justify their respective religious and political views. This consequently led to the development of the science of verification and authentication of *hadīth* later in this era. Also, there was more recourse to *ijtihād* and rationalism (*raʾy*) in addressing the complex issues of the time. The Umayyads favoured legal pragmatism over religious idealism, which they justified within the context of Islamic sources in relation to the challenges of their era. While the Umayyad rulers claimed adherence to Islamic norms, they were criticized by some of the clergy as deviating from orthodox Islamic teachings. Towards the last decades of Umayyad rule, there emerged different fraternities of Muslim scholars and jurists who expressed jurisprudential opinions on the different issues of the time. They included great jurists like Imām Abū Ḥanīfah (699–767 CE) in Kūfa and Imām Mālik ibn Anas (711–95 CE) in

Madīnah, with the former later becoming the eponym of the Hanafī School and the latter the eponym of the Mālikī School of Islamic jurisprudence.

Islamic judicial administration improved significantly under the Umayyads, with legal development in areas such as fiscal, market, and land regulations, judicial administration, and protection of non-Muslim subjects. In discussing this development Noel Coulson argued that elements of Persian and Roman norms infiltrated into the practice of Islamic law during the period, noting, for example, that the Islamic rules governing non-Muslim subjects established at the time were modelled largely on Roman law. To the contrary, other Western scholars such as Montgomery Watt and Muslim historians traced the Islamic rules on protection of non-Muslim subjects back to the Prophet's time, based on the concept of *jiwār* (neighbourhood) or *dhimmah* derived from the traditional Arab custom of stronger tribes protecting weaker tribes and incorporated into Islamic law through religious approval. Despite the political shortcomings of the Umayyads, it is acknowledged that they laid an implementational groundwork for Islamic law, which was consolidated by the Abbāsids who assumed political power after them.

The Abbāsids overthrew the Umayyads in 750 CE and moved the seat of government from Damascus to Baghdad in 762 CE. To demonstrate their commitment to upholding Islamic ideals, the Abbāsids gave formal recognition to the Islamic clergy by consulting them regularly about the different challenges of the time. Meanwhile, different cities such as Madīnah and Makkah in the Arabian Peninsula, Basrā and Kūfa in Iraq, Damascus in Syria, and Fustāt in Egypt had developed into important centres of Islamic learning and jurisprudence. They represented the early geographic jurisprudential centres preceding the formal individual jurisprudential schools that emerged later. Of these centres Madīnah and Kūfa proved to be the most important and enduring, with the different environments impacting the views of the respective jurists of each centre. The Madīnan jurists mostly had a conservative attachment to Prophetic traditions as a validating source of Islamic law, with little tolerance for rational jurisprudence. They were thus referred to as *ahl al-hadīth* (Traditionalists). Conversely, the Kūfan jurists were relatively liberal and, while adhering to Prophetic traditions, were motivated by their cosmopolitan environment to also accommodate the spirit of free enquiry and rational jurisprudence, whenever necessary. They were thus referred to as *ahl al-ra'y* (Rationalists). Joseph Schacht argued that the development of legal theory in the 2nd century of Islam was dominated by the struggle between these two groups of jurists, with Christopher Melchert proposing that there was great animosity between these two groups at the time. However, Muslim legal historians contend that the juristic differences at the time were not clearly divided along geographic lines as there was a mixture of jurists leaning either towards Traditionalism or Rationalism in each of the regions. They argued that the differences between the Traditionalists and Rationalists were not as bitter as suggested by Melchert, rather the jurists engaged with each other in mutual respect despite their differences.

One of the greatest jurists during Abbāsid rule was Abū 'Abdillāh Muhammad ibn Idrīs al-Shāfi'ī, popularly known as Imām al-Shāfi'ī, who was born in 767 CE at the peak of the jurisprudential difference between the Traditionalists and Rationalists. He grew up in Makkah and studied under the leading jurists there. He later moved to Madīnah and studied under Imām Mālik who was the leading jurist of Madīnah. After that, he moved to Iraq, where he studied in Baghdad under the students of Imām Abū Hanīfah, including Imām Muhammad al-Shaybāni, and was exposed to the legal reasoning of the Iraqi jurists. He subsequently moved to Egypt where he reformulated his legal opinions and founded a new school by synthesizing the Traditionalist and Rationalist juristic approaches. He then formulated his famous jurisprudential treatise, *al-risālah fī usūl al-fiqh*, in which he devised a formal legal theory on the sources and methods of Islamic law through a combination of text and reasoning in identifying the law. It is recognized as the first formal jurisprudential work to offer a consistent theoretical framework for textual interpretation and legal reasoning in Islamic law that endures till today.

Essentially, this was the era of the classical jurists who formalized Islamic jurisprudence (*fiqh*) and its theoretical principles (*usūl al-fiqh*) that are still applicable today. Some of the leading jurists of this period were Imām Abū Hanīfah (699–767 CE), Imam Mālik ibn Anas (711–95 CE), Imām Muhammad al-Shāfiʿī (767–820 CE), and Imām Ahmad ibn Hanbal (780–855 CE). These jurists were the eponyms of the four main *Sunnī* jurisprudential schools that have survived until today. There also emerged different *Shīʿah* jurisprudential schools, the major ones being the Ithnā Asharī, the Zaydī, and the Ismāʿilī jurisprudential schools.

By the end of this period, Islamic law and legal institutions had evolved significantly in four main areas, namely: (i) emergence of a systemized Islamic legal methodology; (ii) a formalized judiciary and court system; (iii) appointment of Imām Abū Yūsuf as the first chief justice (*qādī al-qudāt*) by the Abbāsid caliph, Harūn Rashīd; (iv) development of positivist legal doctrine and compilation of basic legal codes such as *kitāb al-kharrāj*, an Islamic revenue code written by Imām Abū Yūsuf at the request of caliph Harūn Rashīd, and *al-ahkām al-sultāniyyah wa al-wilāyāt al-dīniyyah*, a code on Islamic rules of governance and religious authority written by Abū al-Hassan al-Māwardī. Some of the legal institutions established during this period were *qādī* courts overseen by the chief justice, office of the inspector of markets and trades (*muhtasib*), police chief (*sāhib al-shurtah*), and a grievance tribunal (*dīwān al-mazālim*). Ibn Khaldūn chronicled in his 14th-century prologue, *al-muqaddimah*, that the office of the police chief 'was originally created by the Abassid dynasty' with two main duties, 'firstly, to concern himself with crimes in the investigating stage, and, secondly, to execute the legal punishments'.

The evolution of Islamic law during this era was legitimized partly through the doctrine of *siyāsah*, which confers upon rulers ample executive political authority to, in their application of Islamic law, consider the practical circumstances and best interest (*maslahah*) of the Muslim polity and populace. This is based on Q4:59—'O you believers, obey God and obey the Messenger and those in authority amongst you…', which is often cited as legal authority for the political doctrine of *siyāsah shar'iyyah* to facilitate good governance (*siyāsah 'ādilah*) as opposed to bad governance (*siyāsah ẓālimah*) in Islamic jurisprudential writings.

The post-classical period

This era began towards the latter part of the Abbāsid period through to the eventual sack of the last Abbāsid caliph by the Mongols in 1258 and subsequently the establishment of the Ottoman Empire by the Ottoman Turks around 1299, lasting up to the late 18th century. This is often referred to as the period of non-Arab Muslim rule which further expanded the application of Islamic law beyond Arab civilization. This period witnessed disintegration in the Islamic empire, with autonomous caliphs ruling in places like Egypt, Yemen, Baghdad, Spain, India, and Syria. It is often seen as the period of stagnation in Islamic law, when the idea of the so-called 'closing of the gate of *ijtihād*' was floated to preserve the classical jurisprudential heritage of Islamic law from being distorted, particularly by the Mongols, who had introduced their tribal systems into Baghdad and other places they conquered within the Islamic empire.

Due to the political situation of the period, Islamic jurisprudence became more conservative, slowing down the evolution of *ijtihād*. While emphasis shifted mainly to following precedents from the classical period, qualified jurists still gave *fatāwā* on new issues that arose during this period. Islamic legal scholarship turned mostly to studying and analysing the methodologies of the different classical jurisprudential schools and jurists. The study of comparative jurisprudence (*fiqh al-ikhtilāf*) became widespread, whereby the different jurisprudential views of the classical jurists were scrutinized and the views that conformed with practical realities of the period were preferred and adopted. The jurists of this period confined themselves mostly to writing commentaries on the jurisprudential works of the classical jurists. This continued until the 19th century Tanzīmāt reforms under the Ottoman Empire from 1839 to 1876. The Tanzīmāt reforms were influenced by European interactions with the Ottoman Empire and intended to transform the empire and its legal system to conform with the state of the time within the limits of Islamic sources.

Scholars such as Wael Hallaq have argued that Islamic law was not really stagnant at the time and that the gate of *ijtihād* was not closed. Rather, the jurists were exercising *ijtihād* within the context of *takhayyur* (eclecticism), *talfīq* (patching-up), and *istihsan* (juristic preference) by relying on the works of the classical jurists but exercising *ijtihād* in choosing which jurisprudential views to adopt amongst the different views of the classical jurists.

The modern period

The modern period of Islamic law is perceived to have started from the mid-19th century with the Tanzīmāt reform movement under the Ottoman Empire and through the efforts of Muslim scholars such as Jamāluddīn al-Afghānī (1838–97), who is perceived as the leading proponent of Islamic legal reform of the late 19th century, and Muhammad Abduh (1849–1905) and Rashīd Ridā (1865–1935), both of whom built on al-Afghānī's Islamic reform ideas. This was part of what became known as the

Islamic 'reform project' (*al-harakah al-islāhiyyah*) instigated by the impact of European advancement and effects of modernity in the Muslim world and on Islamic thought. It was propelled by the juristic argument that the gate of *ijtihād* was not closed or if it was then it should be reopened to facilitate the required engagement of Islamic law with the challenges of modernity.

Oussama Arabi noted that three main imperatives influenced modern Islamic legal reform from the 19th century, namely, the need 'for greater unity, coherence and efficiency of the law; for a proper Islamic legal identity which would meet the challenges of the time while not renouncing the fundamental gains of the past; and for the elements of modern power and social progress, as exemplified by European nations'. These challenges paved the way for a variety of jurisprudential engagements and theories by different contemporary Muslim jurists and scholars of the 20th century who have been striving to evolve a new Islamic legal theory out of the traditional rules in response to the social realities that confront Islamic law in modern times. Hallaq has provided a useful analysis of these modern jurisprudential efforts in a chapter titled: 'Crises of modernity: towards a new theory of law?' in his epic work titled *A History of Islamic Legal Theories*. This effort underlies the advancement of the idea for a modern *usūl-al-fiqh* as a new jurisprudential methodology for moving Islamic law forward and making it compatible with the demands of modernity and the dynamics of human life.

An emerging post-modern period of Islamic law?

A post-modern period of Islamic law seems to be emerging in the 21st century. This is consequent to the al-Qaeda terrorist act of 11 September 2001 in the United States of America, based on distorted interpretations of Islamic sources supported by other terrorist groups such as ISIS, Al-Shabab, and Boko Haram in different parts of the world. This has put the *sharī'ah* and Islamic law under severe global interrogation, challenging contemporary Muslim scholars and jurists to counteract that hostile ideology wrongly attributed to Islam.

Building on both classical and contemporary Islamic jurisprudence, contemporary Muslim scholars and jurists such as Muhammad Hashim Kamali, Khaled Abou El Fadl, Yūsuf al-Qardāwī, and Abdallah bin Bayyah amongst others, are jurisprudentially repudiating that atrocious ideology as being contrary to the benevolent objectives of the *sharī'ah*. There is laudable scholarly effort to promote a renewed compassionate understanding and application of Islamic law globally. The doctrine of *maqāsid al-sharī'ah* (objectives of the *sharī'ah*) and principle of *maslahah* (human welfare) have both been brought to the forefront in the works of contemporary Islamic scholars in arguing that the underlying objective of the *sharī'ah* and Islamic law is to ensure human well-being and global peace.

This signifies a new positive post-modern evolution of Islamic law for the 21st century and beyond. An evolution underpinned by benevolence, human dignity, human cooperation, global justice, and international peace and security as enjoined by Qur'anic provisions such as Q16:90—'God enjoins the doing of justice and the doing of good [to others]...and He forbids indecency, evil and rebellion; He admonishes you that you may be mindful', Q5:2—'...cooperate in goodness and righteousness and do not cooperate in sin and aggression and be God-conscious...', and Q7:56—'And do not create mischief on earth after its perfection, and call on Him [God] in fear and hope; surely God's mercy is near to those who do good [to others]'.

Evidently, Islamic law has not been static since its inception in the 7th century. Rather, its theories and methodologies have evolved for more than fourteen centuries and will, as a matter of necessity, continue to evolve into the future to remain relevant as an applicable legal system, particularly in the Muslim world.

Chapter 2
The nature of Islamic law

Understanding the nature of Islamic law relates to Islamic legal theory (*usūl al-fiqh*). Many Muslims often claim casually that Islamic law is the 'law of God' in contrast to secular law as 'man-made law', which suggests that Islamic law is completely divine, ready-made, with no human input at all. This usually arises from the non-distinction between the sources, methods, and principles of Islamic law. It is important to appreciate that while Islamic law is based textually on immutable divine sources, its interpretation and application are based on mutable human jurisprudence. The distinction between the law and its sources is carefully maintained in Islamic jurisprudence because the law is not entirely self-evident but buried within the divine sources and has to be extracted from the sources through human effort called *ijtihād*. This point is well illustrated by the 12th-century Islamic jurist, Abū Hāmid Al-Ghazālī, in his book on Islamic legal theory, *al-mustasfā min 'ilm al-usūl*, wherein he emphasizes the need to appreciate the jurists' role of extracting the law from the divine sources. He metaphorically described the law as fruits (*thamarāt*) that must be derived from the fruit source (*al-muthammir*) by a qualified jurist (*mujtahid*) acting as its harvester (*mustathmir*). The jurist exerts his reasoning sincerely in understanding the divine sources according to established human methods. However, Islamic law is also not completely secular, as the practice of *ijtihād* must always be within the context of the divine sources.

Jurisprudentially, Islamic law can be perceived either from a historical or an evolutional perspective. Perceiving it in a strict historical perspective restricts it to traditional jurisprudence and represents it as a static legal system stuck in the past, not responsive to the dynamics of human life. That perspective often ignores that Islamic law has evolved significantly in theory and practice over the past fourteen centuries and is still evolving. Some advocates of that perspective construe the evolution of Islamic law as a 'secularization' process contrary to the 'true' Islamic legal tradition. Conversely, the evolutional perspective acknowledges its traditional jurisprudence but also its theoretical and practical evolution as an inherent part of the Islamic legal process and tradition. That perspective provides a functional understanding of Islamic law based on its historical foundations, development, and transformations in response to the dynamics of life within the objectives of its divine sources. Joseph Schacht aptly identified that:

> Although Islamic law is a 'sacred law', it is by no means essentially irrational; it was created not by an irrational process of continuous revelation but by a rational method of interpretation, and the religious standards and moral rules which were introduced into the legal subject-matter provided the framework for its structural order.

There are three main interconnected questions relating to the nature of Islamic law, namely: (i) Is Islamic law really 'Law'? (ii) Does Islamic law apply only to devotional matters? And (iii) Is Islamic law completely divine and immutable?

Is Islamic law really 'Law'?

The question is often asked, especially by Western lawyers, whether Islamic law can be properly considered as 'Law'. This question has become more topical due to the continuing incorporation of aspects of Islamic law into state law in most modern Muslim-majority countries and in some Muslim-minority secular countries today. There are three main views on this question.

First, there is the view that Islamic law is just a system of religious norms not meant to be legally enforced as law. Advocates of this view argue, *inter alia*, that the modern state, as the main coercive law-making institution today, was unknown within classical Islamic jurisprudence. This represents a circumscribed conception of 'Law', which can be contested on grounds that the nature of Islamic law as 'Law' cannot be based on the presumption that 'Law' only occurs within the coercive powers of the modern state. It also suggests that early Muslim society was a primitive society that had no formal 'Laws' regulating its affairs, which is also empirically false. Second, there is the view that Islamic law is indeed 'Law'. Advocates of this view make empirical reference to its practical application as 'Law' during the Prophet's era in Madīnah, followed by the succeeding caliphs after him and its evolution in the different eras analysed in Chapter 1. Today, aspects of Islamic law are applied as part of state law in different Muslim-majority countries. Islamic law is also taught in the law faculties of different universities in the Muslim world where prospective Islamic lawyers and judges are trained. Islamic courts that apply Islamic law as 'Law' also exist in different parts of the Muslim world today. This empirical view is, however, challenged, for example, by Abdullahi An-Na'im's assertion that the mere claim by states to be Islamic is not sufficient reason to concede the claim, and that 'whatever the state enforces is not shari'a'. The third view is that, unlike other legal systems that claim to separate law and morality, Islamic law does not strictly separate law from morals or ethics and thus its strength actually lies in blending the moral and ethical into the legal. This view asserts that having a religious source does not divest Islamic law of its nature as 'Law' in a true legal sense.

While Islamic theology and ethics do influence Islamic law significantly, Islamic law is distinct from Islamic theology or mere ethics. The classical Islamic jurists had divided Islamic jurisprudence into justiciable matters and non-justiciable matters. For example, the 12th-century Islamic jurist, Ibn Rushd al-Qurtubī, noted in the chapter on judicial practice (*kitāb al-aqḍiyah*) of his jurisprudential opus, *bidāyah al-mujtahid wa nihāyah al-muqtasid*, that there are two types of Islamic jurisprudential rulings—those that are justiciable as law by judges and those not justiciable but in the category of recommended ethical or devotional acts.

Theoretically, the question of whether or not Islamic law is really 'Law' depends on what is meant by 'Law'. Is it the legislation, legal process, judicial decisions, or a combination of all these? Evidently, law is a social fact and every society has its own criteria for identifying what qualifies as law. The Islamic concept of law can be appreciated from Coulson's observation that while his book, *A History of Islamic Law*, 'is confined to law properly so called, the moral scale serves as a reminder of the essentially religious character of the Sharī'a and of the fact that we are here dealing with but one part of a comprehensive guide to conduct, all of which is "law" in the Islamic sense and the ultimate purpose of which is to secure divine favour both in this world and in the hereafter'.

Even in Western legal theory, the debate about what is law is stuck in controversy. There are, *inter alia*, the positivist, naturalist, realist, and functionalist conceptions of law, each of which perceives law differently and has evolved differently over time. In engaging with the general question of what is law, William Twinning refers to H. L. A. Hart's *The Concept of Law*, noting that 'Law' exists under five main conditions, namely that (i) 'This law satisfies the criteria of validity of the legal system of which it is a part', (ii) 'This legal system is formed of a combination of primary and secondary rules', (iii) 'These rules derive their validity from a basic rule of recognition', (iv) 'The rule of recognition is as a matter of social fact accepted as such by the officials of the system', and (v) 'The legal system is effective in the society to which it belongs'. Evidently, Islamic law does satisfy these conditions of 'Law', especially in its application in the Muslim world, and Muslims do acknowledge it as 'Law' properly so called.

Does Islamic law apply only to devotional matters?

The perception of Islamic law as 'religious law' also creates the tendency to presume that it applies only to Islamic devotional matters. This is not so, because the Qur'an and the *Sunnah* contain provisions on both devotional and secular matters. The classical Muslim jurists categorized human acts regulated by the *sharī'ah* into: (i) dogmas/worship (*aqā'id/'ibādāt*), which are essentially theological, (ii) morals (*akhlāq*), which are essentially ethical, (iii) punishments (*'uqūbāt*), and (iv) civil transactions (*mu'āmalāt*), which relate to human social/secular transactions. This can be illustrated with three specific Qur'anic injunctions as follows.

For example, Q3:97 provides that *hajj* pilgrimage is an obligation owed to God by every Muslim who can afford it, but this is not juridically enforceable. Thus, no legal action can be brought against a Muslim who has the means to perform the *hajj* pilgrimage but fails to do so, because it is strictly a devotional obligation owed to God. Similarly, while Q4:86 provides that 'When you are greeted with a greeting, greet in return with what is better, or [at least] return with similar [greeting]; certainly, God takes account of all things', this is strictly a moral injunction that cannot be juridically pursued.

In contrast, Q4:7 provides that there is a legal share of inheritance for both men and women from property left by parents and relations. Unlike the previous devotional and moral injunctions, this provision on inheritance is an injunction relating to a civil right that can be legally and juridically pursued. Thus, a legal action can be brought to enforce it in court if, for example, there is an attempt by one child to exclude other siblings from sharing in their late parent's estate. Similarly, there are specific legal injunctions on crimes and their punishments as analysed in Chapter 7.

However, while devotional, moral, and ethical injunctions of the *sharī'ah* may not be juridically enforceable, their neglect may attract communal criticism. Also, Muslims believe that there may be adverse religious consequences in the hereafter for violators of such divine injunctions.

Is Islamic law completely divine and immutable?

When analysing the nature of Islamic law, it is imperative to distinguish between its divine sources known as *sharī'ah* and its human jurisprudence known as *fiqh*. Jurisprudentially, the term *sharī'ah* refers to the main sources of the law, i.e. the Qur'an and the *Sunnah*, which are divine and textually immutable, while *fiqh* refers to the human understanding and interpretation of the *sharī'ah*, which may change according to time and circumstances. Islamic law is derived from the *sharī'ah* through *fiqh*.

In essence, Islamic law is the rulings (*ahkām*; sing. *hukm*) that are derived from the *sharī'ah* by jurists. Muslim jurists normally talk of '*ahkām al-sharī'ah*' (sing. '*hukm al-sharī'ah*'), i.e. '*sharī'ah* rulings', or '*fiqh Islāmiyy*', i.e. Islamic jurisprudence, when referring to applied Islamic law. The law is extracted through the human juristic process of *ijtihād*, using different jurisprudential methods and principles under Islamic legal theory. Thus, it was through the medium of *fiqh*, based on the process of *ijtihād*, that the early Muslim jurists transformed the *sharī'ah* into applied Islamic law. Anwar Qadri noted the classical jurists' observation that 'though God has given us a revelation He also gave us brains to understand it'. Thus, based on their human understandings of the provisions of the *sharī'ah*, the classical

jurists compiled *fiqh* manuals containing the *ahkām al-sharī'ah*
as expounded by them under different jurisprudential schools.
The jurisprudential rulings are accepted as law, but unlike the
sharī'ah itself, are not immutable.

Notably, Islamic law has always been specified in the context of
fiqh by the jurists as reflected in the titles of their different *fiqh*
manuals. Some well-known examples are al-Jazīrī's *al-fiqh*
alā al-madhāhib al-arba'ah (*Fiqh* according to the four
jurisprudential schools), Sayyid Sābiq's *fiqh al-sunnah* (*Fiqh*
according to the *Sunnah*), and Wahbah al-Zuhaylī's contemporary
al-fiqh al-Islāmiyy wa adillatuh (Islamic *fiqh* and its evidences),
amongst many others. Hammudah 'Abd al 'Atī has observed that
'confusion arises when the term *shariah* is used uncritically to
designate not only the divine law in its pure principal form, but
also its human subsidiary sciences including *fiqh*'. He further
argued that 'those who subscribe to the divine origin and the
unchangeable essence of Islamic law seem to mistake the general
for the variant, that is to view the whole legal system…as identical
with *shariah* in the strict pure sense, [and] those who subscribe
to the…human character of Islamic law seem to view the whole
system as identical with one part thereof, that is *fiqh* which,
strictly speaking is human and socially grounded'.

The main significance of this distinction is that it clarifies that
by its nature Islamic law consists of two component parts: (i)
immutable divine sources termed *sharī'ah* and (ii) human
understanding and interpretation of the *sharī'ah* termed *fiqh*.
The interaction between these two component parts of Islamic
law is the crux of Islamic legal theory, which is further analysed
in Chapter 3.

Chapter 3
Theory, scope, and practice

Similar to other legal systems, Islamic law consists of theoretical, substantive, and procedural aspects. The theoretical aspect engages with the jurisprudential rules relating to the sources, methods, principles, legal hermeneutics, and juristic methodologies of Islamic law. The substantive aspect deals with the scope of Islamic law, covering the textual provisions and juristic rulings on specific substantive issues. The procedural aspect deals with Islamic law in practice, covering its practical application as a functional legal system. Although reference to 'Islamic law' in Western literature often focuses on Islamic legal theory, a holistic understanding requires coverage of all its three aspects as presented in this book.

Islamic legal theory

Islamic legal theory is called '*uṣūl al-fiqh*', literally translated as 'roots of the law'. It engages with the relationship between the divine sources and human reason. Islamic jurists consider it as most essential in relation to the sources, methods, principles, and rules of interpretation in Islamic law.

An informal legal methodology emerged soon after the Prophet's death, through which complex questions not explicated by the Qur'an or *Sunnah* were resolved. For example, the '*iddah* (minimum waiting period before remarrying) of a pregnant widow became unclear during the era of the Prophet's companions, in view of two divergent Qur'anic verses on the issue. Q2:234 states: 'Those who die among you leaving widows behind, they shall observe a waiting period of four months and ten days...', while Q65:4 states: '...and for pregnant women, their waiting period is until they deliver their pregnancy...'. 'Abdullah ibn Mas'ūd resolved the apparent conflict by noting that since Q65:4 was the latter verse and also of general application, it superseded and modified Q2:234 in relation to pregnant widows. Thus, the waiting period of a pregnant widow ended when she delivered her pregnancy. This established the legal principle that a later Qur'anic verse could repeal or modify a former verse on the same subject. There were many such examples during the pre-classical period of Islamic law.

Later, *usūl al-fiqh* was developed as a formal methodology alongside *fiqh* around the 9th century, during the Abbāsid period. Through it, specific legal rules were established for engaging with jurisprudential questions on the sources, hermeneutics, and methodology for discovering and applying the law. Thus, Islamic legal theory deals with the techniques of the law and imparts the skills of *ijtihād*. In his *bidāyah al-mujtahid*, Ibn Rushd likened the Islamic jurist to a skilled cobbler who has the ability to make shoes to fit different sizes of feet at different times rather than the one who merely possesses a large collection of shoes but is unable to fit some feet sometimes. This analogy indicates that the study of Islamic legal theory is not to merely memorize the law but to engage with the context of the law and understand its rules, methodology, and technique for its evolution. It imparts the skills and ability to derive the law from the divine sources and the capacity to understand its objective and application. Similarly, in the introduction of his *al-mustasfā min 'ilm al-usūl*, al-Ghazālī noted that *fiqh* and *usūl al-fiqh* constitute the highest form of legal knowledge, whereby rational opinion (*ra'y*) and the revealed sources (*sharī'ah*) are in alliance. Some distinction is usually

made between *Sunnī* and *Shī'ah* legal theory based on minor
jurisprudential differences between the two groupings.
Nevertheless, there is broad similarity in their approaches and
methodologies generally.

Imām al-Shāfi'ī is acknowledged as the first jurist to have
formulated a systemized scheme of Islamic legal theory during
the classical period of Islamic law. Some scholars argue that the
subject had been addressed by jurists before Imām al-Shāfi'ī.
Coulson noted that Imām al-Shāfi'ī's genius lay 'not in the
introduction of any entirely original concepts, but in giving existing
ideas a novel connotation and emphasis and welding them together
within a systematic scheme'. Essentially, Imām al-Shāfi'ī succeeded
in formulating a systemized hierarchy of sources for Islamic law
by synthesizing both 'text' and 'reasoning' in identifying the law.

Since the classical period, Islamic legal theory has mostly been
presented in the form of descriptive legal theory, often merely
restating the classical rules. Many contemporary jurists have
identified the need for a more normative and adaptive
methodology that engages effectively with contemporary
challenges. Thus, there is continuing scholarly effort towards
the emergence of a refined Islamic legal theory in response to
different legal questions confronting Islamic law in
contemporary times.

Sources of Islamic law

Imām al-Shāfi'ī identified 'four sources' of Islamic law, namely the
Qur'an, the *Sunnah*, *Ijmā'* (consensus), and *Qiyās* (analogy), in
that order of priority. He first established the primacy of the
Qur'an as the ultimate source of Islamic law and went on to justify
each of the other three from the authority of the Qur'an, referring,
inter alia to Q4:59—'O you believers, obey God and obey the
Messenger and those in authority amongst you; and if you differ
in anything refer it back to God and to the Messenger ...'.

Obedience to God and the Messenger means obedience to the Qur'an and the *Sunnah*, while obedience to those in authority means obedience to the rulings of jurists and leaders, who must in turn show that their rulings are in accordance with the Qur'an and the *Sunnah* through either *Ijmā'* or *Qiyās*. Imām al-Shāfi'ī also acknowledged *ijtihād*, *istihsān* (juristic preference), and *ikhtilāf* (juristic differences) as necessary principles of Islamic law in his jurisprudential scheme.

The traditional concept of 'four sources' is now well established in *Sunnī* jurisprudence with some slight variations between the jurisprudential schools regarding the scope of *Ijmā'* and *Qiyās*. Similarly, *Shī'ah* jurisprudence recognizes the concept of 'four sources' but replaces *Qiyās* with *'Aql* (intellect) as the fourth. This traditional conception of the 'four sources' of Islamic law conflates the immutable divine sources with the mutable human methods of the law. To avoid such conflation, Islamic law is better perceived as having two sources, namely, the Qur'an and the *Sunnah*, while *Ijmā'* and *Qiyās* (or *'Aql* in *Shī'ah* jurisprudence) constitute the methods of Islamic law rather than 'sources' in the true sense.

The Qur'an describes itself as a book of guidance (*hudā*) for every aspect of human life, including law, with its verses covering diverse matters, including legal issues. Its legal verses regulate social and secular matters such as trade, inheritance, crimes, etc., some of which are covered in the latter chapters of this book. There is disparity between Muslim jurists and Western scholars about the amount of legal verses in the Qur'an. For example, while Coulson notes that '[n]o more than approximately eighty verses [of the Qur'an] deal with legal topics in the strict sense of the term', Kamali identified that '[t]here are close to 350 legal [verses] in the Qur'an'. Other Muslim jurists identify even a higher number of legal verses.

As a divine source, it is always necessary to ensure correct interpretation of Qur'anic provisions. Prophet Muhammad provided the required interpretation of the Qur'anic verses during his lifetime, but after him the science of exegesis ('*ilm al-tafsīr*) was developed to ensure consistent rules of Qur'anic interpretation. Thus, there are rules of literal and contextual interpretations and identifiable causes of revelation (*asbāb al-nuzūl*) of specific verses to aid the contextual understanding of the verses.

The verses of the Qur'an are classified variously, with defined rules of interpretation and application, into the explicit (*mufassar*), decisive (*muhkamāt*), allegorical (*mutashābihāt*), or ambivalent (*mujmal*). This is hinged on Q3:7—'It is He [God] Who revealed the Book [Qur'an] to you; in it are verses that are decisive (*muhkamāt*), they are the core of the Book, and others that are allegorical (*mutashābihāt*)...'. Other legal classifications include the definitive (*qat'ī*), the speculative (*zannī*), the general ('*āmm*), the particular (*khāss*), the abrogated (*mansūkh*), and the abrogating (*nāsikh*). Also, there are the commanding verses (*awāmir*; sing. *amr*), the prohibiting verses (*nawāhīy*; sing. *nahy*) and the descriptive verses (*akhbār*; sing. *khabar*). Knowledge of all these rules is an important aspect of Islamic legal theory and imperative for a proper interpretation of the legal verses and their purposeful application. The jurists identify that a large number of the legal verses are speculative (*zannī*) in nature, which often leads to different juristic interpretations. Based on these rules, Qur'anic interpretation ranges from the literal to semi-literal and contextual, which are all applicable today within specific rules.

The *Sunnah* complements the Qur'an as a source of law. Coulson noted that the Prophet acquired 'extra-Quranic law-making' capacity through the *Sunnah*. This capacity is not self-acquired but derives from the Qur'an, which enjoins obedience to the Prophet in many places, such as Q4:59—'O you believers, obey God and obey the Messenger...' and Q4:80—'He who obeys the Messenger, indeed obeys God'. The *Sunnah* is based on the Prophet's sayings (*qawlīyyah*), actions (*fi'līyyah*), and tacit approvals (*taqrīrīyyah*) on different issues as reported in *ahādīth*. Imām al-Shāfiʿī asserted in his *al-risālah* that the Prophet's *Sunnah* must be followed because God has ordered us to obey the Prophet and He regards such obedience as obedience to Himself and disobedience to the Prophet as disobedience to Himself. He also noted that the Prophet's *Sunnah* falls into three categories: (i) the *Sunnah* that corroborates Qurʾanic prescriptions, (ii) the *Sunnah* that clarifies ambiguous provisions in the Qurʾan, and (iii) the *Sunnah* that covers issues not specifically covered in the Qurʾan. The other jurists also declare similar categorizations of the *Sunnah*.

Due to the emergence of fabricated *ahādīth* attributed to the Prophet after his death, the science of *hadīth* authentication and classification was developed from the 9th century. With regard to soundness of content, *ahādīth* are classified mainly into authentic (*sahīh*), good (*hasan*), weak (*daʿīf*), and fabricated (*mawdūʿ*) and with regard to strength of transmission, they are classified mainly into widespread (*mutawātir*), well-known (*mashhūr*), solitary (*ahhād*), and broken (*munqatiʿ*). From that process emerged the six canonical *Sunnī hadīth* compilations (*al-sahīh al-sittah*) namely: *Sahīh al-Bukharī* by Imām al-Bukhari (d. 870 CE); *Sahīh Muslim* by Imām Muslim (d. 875 CE); *Sunan Abī Dāwūd* by Imām Abū Dāwūd (d. 888 CE); *Sunan al-Nasāʾī* by Imām al-Nasāʾī (d. 915 CE); *Jāmiʿ al-Tirmidhī* by Imām al-Tirmidhī (d. 892 CE); and *Sunan Ibn Mājah* by Imām Ibn Mājah (d. 886 CE), which serve as sources of recorded authentic *Sunnah* for Islamic law today in *Sunnī* legal theory (see Figure 5).

The *Shīʿah* also have their own different collections of traditions, called *akhbār*, that serve as the second source of Islamic law under *Shīʿah* legal theory. The fundamental principle is that the *akhbār* transmitted by the *Shīʿah* Imāms are regarded as the most authentic source of the *Sunnah* in *Shīʿah* legal theory. The four main recognized books of *Shīʿah* traditions (*al-kutub al-arbaʿah*) are *al-kāfi fī ʿilm al-dīn* by Shaykh al-Kulaynī (d. 940 CE), *man lā yahduruhū al-faqīh* by Shaykh Ibn Bābūya (d. 991 CE), and *tahdhīb al-aḥkām* and *al-istibsār fī mā ukhtulifa minhu al-akhbār* by Shaykh al-Ṭūsī (d. 1067 CE).

Western scholarship has challenged the status of the *Sunnah* as a source of Islamic law and the reliability of *ḥadīth* as its vehicle. For example, Joseph Schacht argued that the Prophet did not intend to institute his *Sunnah* as a source of law and that *aḥādīth* were arbitrarily back-projected to the Prophet after his death in ways that were not theoretically objective or historically reliable. This contention has been challenged generally by other scholars, with Wael Hallaq noting that despite the different approaches adopted by the scholars, 'they all share one fundamental assumption, namely, that the early and medieval Muslim scholars

5. A nine-volume English language translation of *Sahīh al-Bukhārī*, which is the leading compilation of authentic Prophetic Traditions (*ahādith*) under *Sunni* jurisprudence.

espoused the view that the Prophetic *hadīth* literature is substantially genuine, and that despite the relatively large scale forgery that took place in the early period, the literature, at least as it came to be constituted in the six so-called canonical collections, has been successfully salvaged and finally proven to be authentic'.

Despite the debate about authenticity and reliability, the authority of the *Sunnah* as a source of Islamic law, after the Qur'an, is well established within Islamic legal scholarship. As noted by Mohammad Nadwi, '[i]n the Qur'an and *Sunnah*, Muslims believe they have a framework of guidance that is strictly impartial and sufficient, because God's knowledge and mercy encompass all beings and all their pasts and futures. Any human derivation from and within that framework is subject to revision, but the framework itself is not.'

Methods of Islamic law

Ijmā' (consensus) and *Qiyās/'Aql* (analogy/intellect) constitute the two methods of Islamic law. Both are human endeavours for expanding the two divine sources. The Prophet's death brought an end to Qur'anic revelations and any new *Sunnah*. With the passage of time and in response to different legal questions raised by new cases that were not specifically covered by the Qur'an or the *Sunnah*, the concepts of *Ijmā'* and *Qiyās/'Aql* were ascertained as complementing rational methods to facilitate the coherent extension of the two divine sources to answer new legal questions into the future.

Ijmā' is the consensus of qualified Muslim jurists, especially on an issue that is not specifically covered in the Qur'an or the *Sunnah*. Where qualified Muslim jurists unanimously agree on a ruling within the general provisions of the *sharī'ah*, such juristic consensus becomes the binding rule on that particular issue. Traditionally, *Ijmā'* is as binding as the Qur'an and *Sunnah*, but unlike the Qur'an and *Sunnah*, an *Ijmā'* may be modified or changed by another valid *Ijmāʿ* of a similar class. There is, however, a view that established *Ijmāʿ* of the Prophet's companions (*ijmāʿ al-sahābah*) cannot be changed after them because it is impossible to create an *Ijmāʿ* of a similar class after them.

Ijmāʿ is justified by reference to Qur'anic verses such as Q3:102— 'And hold fast altogether to the covenant of God and be not divided...' and *ahādīth* that enjoin Muslims to hold together as a community, especially a *hadīth* in which the Prophet said: 'God will not unite my community upon an error' (al-Tirmidhī). However, there are juristic differences on the practical formation of *Ijmāʿ*. George Hourani has noted that although *Ijmāʿ* is a well-established method of Islamic law, there are jurisprudential debates around questions such as '[w]hat was the constituting group whose unanimous opinion was binding: the entire community or [just] the learned?' In his *al-risālah*, Imām al-Shāfiʿī held the view that *Ijmāʿ* meant the consensus of the entire Muslim community not just jurists. To the contrary, the Hanafīs limited it to the consensus of jurists, while the Mālikīs restricted it to the consensus of the residents of Madīnah, and the Hanbalīs limited it to the consensus of the Prophet's companions during their time. For the *Shīʿah*, *Ijmāʿ* is restricted to the consensus of their Imāms. Today, most contemporary jurists are of the view that *Ijmāʿ* can be achieved through the consensus of qualified jurists of a particular jurisdiction at a particular time on a matter relating to that particular jurisdiction and time.

Despite these juristic differences, *Ijmāʿ* is generally recognized as a valid method of Islamic law under both *Sunnī* and *Shīʿah* legal theory, but with some theoretical and practical differences between them in respect of its scope of application.

Qiyās consists of the juristic extension of an original provision from the Qur'an or *Sunnah* to cover, by analogy, a new case for which a legal ruling is required. It has four elements: (i) existence of an original rule *(asl)* prescribed by the Qur'an or *Sunnah*; (ii) occurrence of a new case *(far')* for which a legal ruling is required; (iii) identification of a logical element or *ratio legis ('illah)* linking the new case to the original rule; and (iv) extending the original ruling *(hukm)* to the new case. This is usually illustrated by reference to the prohibition of narcotics under Islamic law by analogy to the prohibition of intoxicating wine *(khamr)* contained in Q5:90 on grounds that narcotics have a similar effect to intoxicating wine on the intellect. The *'illah* is an important element that must be objectively established for a valid application of *Qiyās* as a method of Islamic law.

The authority for *Qiyās* is based on Qur'anic verses such as Q3:13—'... certainly, there is a lesson for those who possess vision' and to the *Sunnah* such as a *hadīth* in which 'Umar ibn al-Khaṭṭāb had asked the Prophet whether kissing his wife vitiated his fast and the Prophet answered him analogically by asking him whether mouth-rinsing with water would vitiate a person's fast, to which 'Umar answered in the negative. The Prophet thus answered 'Umar's question by analogy. Apparently, Imām al-Shāfi'ī's aim for accommodating *Qiyās* was to restrict the free usage of rationality *(ra'y)* without textual limitation. He argued that no one is competent to apply *Qiyās* except a jurist with in-depth knowledge of the Qur'an and the *Sunnah*. The concept of *Qiyās* is quite technical and requires some expertise in logic, which makes its analysis sometimes difficult. Also, while *Qiyās* is mostly reflected as analogical deduction, some early jurists recognized its possible application in other circumstances, resulting in jurisprudential debates about different types of *Qiyās*.

As previously noted, *Qiyās* is only recognized as a method of Islamic law under *Sunnī* jurisprudence, but substituted with the concept of *'Aql* (intellect) under *Shī'ah* jurisprudence. The concept of *'Aql* may be defined as free intellectualism not textually limited like *Qiyās*. The *Shī'ah* consider *'Aql* as more definitive compared to *Qiyās* which they consider too tentative. Within *Sunnī* jurisprudence there are juristic differences regarding the scope and usage of *Qiyās*. The Hanafīs and Mālikīs have strong support for *Qiyās*, while the Shāfiʿīs accept it with caution and the Hanbalīs try to avoid using it whenever possible.

The interplay between the sources and methods of Islamic law is a very significant aspect of Islamic legal theory. Imām al-Shāfiʿī had carefully systemized the relationship between the two in an effort to resolve the jurisprudential differences that arose between the Traditionalists and Rationalists during his time.

Principles of Islamic law

The practical application of the sources and methods of Islamic law is guided by established jurisprudential principles (*qawāʾid*), especially under *Sunnī* legal theory. This is aimed at ensuring consistency between theory and practice and a sensible application of the law. Examples of established principles of Islamic law include *ḍarūrah* (necessity), *maslahah* (welfare or public interest), and *istihsān* (juristic preference). All the principles are justified by reference to relevant provisions of the Qurʾan and *Sunnah*.

Ḍarūrah is the principle of necessity, which enables proportionate divergence from the letter of the law in cases of compelling necessity or duress. This principle finds authority in six Qurʾanic verses, namely, Q2:173—'…whoever is driven by necessity, neither desiring nor exceeding the limit, no sin shall be upon him; certainly God is Most-forgiving, Most-merciful' and Q5:3; 6:119; 6:145; 16:106; 16:115, each of which contains a similar provision. It is reflected in the legal maxim: 'Necessities permit divergences.' Its application is however balanced by the principle of proportionality reflected in the complementing legal maxim: 'Necessity is limited by its proportion.'

Maslahah is the principle of welfare or public interest, which allows for the consideration of human welfare in the application of Islamic law. It derives its validity from the basic norm that the *sharī'ah* is intended to ensure human welfare. Examples of Qur'anic authority for this principle include Q 5:6—'...God does not desire to impose hardship upon you' and Q2:185—'...God desires ease for you and He does not desire hardship for you.' Another authority is the *hadīth* 'Let there be no harm or reciprocation of harm' (Ibn Mājah). This principle reflects the underlying purpose of the *sharī'ah* and thus the provisions of the Qur'an and *Sunnah* must not be interpreted to contradict it. *Maslahah* is often considered as the most viable principle for bringing the humane ideals of Islamic law closer to realization for all time.

Istihsān is derived from '*ahsan*' (better or best) and it is the principle of juristic preference which enables judges to be fair and equitable, based on the facts before them, by choosing the most benevolent amongst different juristic views on a particular matter. Two relevant Qur'anic authorities for this principle are Q39:18—'Those who listen to the word, then follow the best of it are the ones whom God has guided and those it is who are of understanding' and Q39:55—'And follow the best of what has been revealed to you from your Lord...'. While the Hanafī, Mālikī, and Hanbalī Schools approve of *istihsān*, the Shāfi'ī, Shī'ah, and Zāhirī Schools reject it. Although Imām al-Shāfi'ī discussed the principle of *istihsān* in his *al-risālah*, he was of the view that it must be exercised only by qualified jurists with reference to specific textual authority from the Qur'an or *Sunnah*.

Other recognized principles include *istishāb* (presumption of continuity), through which subsistence of the status quo is presumed until the contrary is proved; *maqāsid al-sharī'ah* (objective of the *sharī'ah*), which requires that interpretations of the Qur'an and *Sunnah* must always be consistent with the *sharī'ah's* objective of ensuring human welfare; *takhayyur* (eclecticism) and *talfīq* (patching-up), each of which allows movement between or mixing the opinions of the different jurisprudential schools to avoid hardship, where necessary; and *'urf* (custom), which allows application of custom that is not violative of the provisions of the Qur'an or *Sunnah*.

There are many more of these principles, most of which have been formulated into maxims to formalize their scope and application in Islamic law. The five overarching jurisprudential maxims (*al-qawā'id al-kulliyyah al-khams*) being: (i) 'Matters are to be considered in the light of their objectives', (ii) 'Certainty shall not be revoked by doubt', (iii) 'Hardship requires allowance of ease', (iv) 'Harm shall be removed', and (v) 'Custom has the authority of law'. Differences however exist in respect of the degree to which some of the principles are applicable under the different jurisprudential schools.

Independent juristic reasoning (*Ijtihād*)

Ijtihād is an important tool of independent juristic reasoning under Islamic legal theory. It is classically defined as the putting forth of every effort to determine a question of the *sharī'ah* with a degree of probability. It requires a thorough study of the sources, objective reflection, and good faith. It derives its authority from Qur'anic verses such as Q47:24—'Do they not reflect on the Qur'an or are there seals on [their] hearts?' and the Prophet's *Sunnah* such as his approval of Mu'ādh's response that he will exercise his personal juristic reasoning (*ajtahidu ra'īy*) in case he found no specific answer to a matter in the Qur'an or *Sunnah*. In illustrating the indispensability of *ijtihād* in his *al-risālah*, Imām al-Shāfi'ī referred to the injunction in Q2:150—'And from wherever you come forth, turn your face towards the sacred mosque; and wherever you all are, turn your faces towards it [in prayer]...', requiring Muslims to turn their faces towards the sacred mosque (*ka'bah*) when praying. He argued that for those in the vicinity of the sacred mosque, there is no difficulty in finding its direction as they can visibly see it. But those not in its vicinity can only seek its direction through exercising *ijtihād* relying on different landmarks to speculatively determine its direction with a degree of probability.

Through *ijtihād*, qualified jurists known as *mujtahidūn* (sing. *mujtahid*) exert sincere effort to derive the law from the divine sources. This includes using *Ijmā* and *Qiyās/ʿAql* to formulate a ruling based on evidence from the divine sources or filling a legal lacuna in the textual sources. It also includes determining the use of principles, such as *maslahah*, *ḍarūrah*, *istihsān*, etc., to resolve any juristic challenges in the application of the law. A qualified *mujtahid* is expected to be a pious person well versed in Qur'anic sciences, the *Sunnah*, and other relevant knowledge related to *ijtihād*. There are different levels of *ijtihād* and *mujtahidūn* based on qualifications and knowledge. The first level is that of full *ijtihād* (*ijtihād fī al-sharʿ*) covering all aspects of the *sharīʿah*, the second level is that of relative *ijtihād* (*ijtihād fī al-madhhab*) covering only a particular jurisprudential school, and the third level is that of specific *ijtihād* (*ijtihād fī al-mas'alah*) covering only a specific issue of Islamic law.

As *ijtihād* is independent juristic reasoning based on a degree of probability, Islamic legal theory also acknowledges the principle of *ikhtilāf* (differences in juristic views) on particular issues, subject to clear evidence (*dalīl*) in support of respective views. This is reflected in the differences of opinion often expressed by jurists of the different jurisprudential schools on most matters. To demonstrate the speculative nature of *ijtihād*, Imām al-Shāfiʿī is reported to have stated that while he was convinced of the veracity of his opinions he was also conscious of the possibility of being wrong, and while he may differ from another juristic view, he was conscious of the possibility of that view being right. The opposite of *ijtihād* is *taqlīd*, which means legal conformism, whereby a layperson follows the opinion of a qualified *mujtahid* on a particular matter.

The notion of the so-called 'closing of the gate of *ijtihād*' is said to have emerged from around the 10th to 13th century. This is claimed to have permanently curtailed the practice of *ijtihād* and limited Islamic law to the practice of *taqlīd* by following the rulings of the classical jurists on different issues as recorded in their classical *fiqh* manuals. This, in essence, represents Islamic law as a system stuck in the past. This so-called 'closing of the gate of *ijtihād*' has been challenged by contemporary scholars and jurists, citing relevant classical sources and practices to establish that *ijtihād* never ceased fully at any time in Islamic legal history. While *taqlīd* remains a necessary methodology of Islamic law to enable laypersons to follow the views of qualified *mujtahidūn*, a qualified *mujtahid* or judge must exercise his own *ijtihād*, in accordance with the *sharī'ah*, in every case before him, with a clear elaboration of the relevant legal methodologies utilized in reaching his decision so that the validity of his judgment can be properly evaluated within the established rules.

It is often suggested that *Shī'ah* jurisprudence was more accommodating of *ijtihād* because of its recognition of *'Aql* (intellect) as a method of Islamic law. This is not necessarily so, as *ijtihād* is equally strongly established within *Sunnī* jurisprudence. A relevant Islamic legal maxim in that regard states that: 'Changes in legal rulings are not proscribed with changes in time and place.' This is currently reflected in the practices of most Muslim-majority countries and communities, as well as in the views of contemporary Muslim jurists and scholars globally. In contemporary times *ijtihād* has occurred mostly in the form of statutory legislation by states, judicial decision by courts, and learned opinion (*fatwā*) by jurisconsults (*muftīs*).

The role of Islamic legal theory as a necessary methodology in the development of Islamic law cannot be overemphasized. From the time of Imām al-Shāfi'ī, when its rules were considered to have been synthesized into a coherent system, it has evolved into an indispensable discipline of Islamic law through which Islamic scholars and jurists have sought to advance Islamic law to meet the various legal challenges of their time. Apart from classical Islamic literature on the subject, there is no doubt that critical contemporary Western scholarship in different aspects of the discipline has contributed to generating a vibrant engagement with its traditional perspectives. The academic debate emerging therefrom has resulted in a more broad-minded approach on the different issues, which has greatly enriched the discipline in recent times. It is important to note that Islamic legal theory cannot, however, apply in a vacuum but in relation to the substantive aspects of the law.

Islamic substantive law

Islamic substantive law is called '*furū' al-fiqh*', literally translated as 'branches of the law', and covers specific substantive issues such as family law, criminal law, etc. It is with regard to substantive law that al-Ghazālī metaphorically described the Islamic jurist as a 'harvester' who uses the rules of Islamic legal theory to harvest the law regulating specific issues from the sources.

Muslim jurists trace the foundations of Islamic substantive law to the Prophet's lifetime when his companions would ask him questions about specific issues and he provided rulings, either by reference to the Qur'an or his own *Sunnah*. This was further developed through juristic reasoning on new issues and questions that arose after the Prophet's time. The traditional process of determining a legal ruling on any issue was that a jurist would first search whether there was a specific Qur'anic provision on the issue, followed, if necessary, by a search for a known *Sunnah* on the issue, and then followed, if necessary, by a search for any evidence of *Ijmā'* on the issue. In the absence of any specific evidence from those three, recourse would then be to *Qiyās* under *Sunnī* jurisprudence or to *'Aql* under *Shī'ah* jurisprudence. This necessarily involves the direct or indirect exercise of *ijtihād* throughout the process. The development of Islamic substantive law was both doctrinal and technical, based on the rules of Islamic legal theory. Also, judges and jurisconsults contributed to the process through their legal decisions and learned opinions respectively. Thus, the development of Islamic substantive law has been influenced by the theoretical constructs of jurists as well as practical realities reflected in judicial decisions and *fatāwā*.

Wael Hallaq has challenged the view of some Western scholars who claimed that Islamic substantive law was based on speculative constructs formulated by the jurists. He noted 'the fact that substantive law embodied in the *furū'* works was, by and large, nothing less than an active organ functioning within a vibrant social environment' and concluded that this questions 'the widely accepted thesis [in Western scholarship] that Islamic law began only towards the end of the first century of Islam and that Muhammad and the generation that followed him did not view themselves as promulgators of Islamic legal norms'.

The scope of Islamic substantive law covers a wide range of private and public law issues. It starts with relevant definitive Qur'anic and *hadīth* provisions that serve as textual sources for juristic rulings on some specific issues. Its scope expands as questions on new substantive issues are raised from time to time and jurisprudentially ruled upon by qualified jurists. Thus, this branch of Islamic law substantially falls within the realm of *fiqh*, based on evidences drawn by qualified jurists from the divine sources, with their respective rulings compiled in the *fiqh* manuals of the different jurisprudential schools.

Most classical *fiqh* manuals would first list the substantive rulings on acts of worship (*'ibādāt*) followed by the substantive rulings on social transactions (*mu'āmalāt*), which represent Islamic substantive law in the strict legal sense. For example, Volume 1 of Ibn Rushd's *bidāyah al-mujtahid* covers rulings on different acts of worship, while its Volume 2 contains the substantive law relating to social transactions such as marriage, divorce, sales, exchange, advance, hire, crop-sharing, partnership, pre-emption, security, interdiction, insolvency, negotiation, surety, debt transfer, agency, bailment, loan, usurpation, restitution, gifts, bequests, inheritance, manumission, crimes and punishments, adjudication, etc. (see Figure 6). In response to current developments, contemporary Islamic jurisprudential works, such as Wahbah al-Zuhaylī's *al-fiqh al-Islamīyy wa adillatuh*, contain, in addition to traditional issues usually covered in the classical manuals, chapters on contemporary issues such as systems of governance and separation of powers. Both the classical and contemporary *fiqh* manuals are consulted as legal references on these matters by Islamic jurists and courts in many Muslim-majority countries today. Also, there is, today, a great deal of Islamic law literature in the English language covering different Islamic substantive issues of contemporary significance.

6. A two-volume English language translation of the 12th-century Mālikī jurist Ibn Rushd's classical comparative Islamic jurisprudential manual, *Bidāyah al-mujtahid wa nihāyah al-muqtasid*.

Six main areas of Islamic substantive law of contemporary relevance, namely, family law; law of inheritance; law of financial transactions; penal law; international law; and administration of justice are briefly analysed in the following chapters.

Islamic law in practice

As analysed in Chapter 1, Islamic law has been in practice amongst Muslims since the time of Prophet Muhammad. Building on the Prophet's practices and the exigencies of their time, the classical Muslim jurists laid down relevant rules on administration of justice and practice of Islamic law which have evolved over time. Today, Islamic law continues to apply variably as part of state law in Muslim-majority countries with reformed rules of procedure to facilitate the substantive justice advocated by the *sharīʿah*. This is further analysed in Chapters 9 and 10.

Chapter 4
Family law

Currently, Islamic family law applies formally as part of state law in all Muslim-majority countries (except Turkey) and also amongst Muslim minorities in other parts of the world. Its two main aspects are: (i) marriage and its legal consequences, and (ii) dissolution of marriage and its legal consequences.

Marriage and its legal consequences

Marriage by mutual contract (*al-nikāh*) is the only lawful type of marriage under Islamic law, with rules regulating its validity and consequences. Legitimacy of *al-nikāh* is found in Qur'anic provisions such as Q4:2—'…marry (*fankihū*) women of your choice…', and *ahādīth* such as 'O young men, whoever among you is able should marry, for it restrains the gaze and guards chastity…' (al-Nasā'ī). Marriage is generally classed as a permissible act (*mubāh*) in Islamic law, however it is legally categorized by the classical jurists according to individual circumstances.

For example, Mālikī jurists deem it obligatory (*fard*) for those fearful of committing fornication (*zinā*); prohibited (*harām*) for those not fearful of committing *zīnā*, who have no sexual urge, or have no means of maintaining a wife (unless the woman is aware of this and consents to it); recommended (*mandūb*) for those with no sexual urge, who are not fearful of committing *zīnā* but want to have children and are able to maintain them; discouraged (*makrūh*) for those with no sexual urge who cannot keep up with the responsibilities of marriage, whether or not they want children; and permissible (*mubāh*) in all other cases. Other jurists hold similar views with slight variations in their respective categorizations of it. Thus, like most acts in Islam, marriage is enjoined only on those who can fulfil its responsibilities.

Based on Qur'anic provisions such as Q30:21—'...He [God] created spouses for you from yourselves that you may find tranquillity in them and He put love and compassion between you...', Islamic jurists assert that the main purposes of marriage are to facilitate mutual support, lawful conjugal relations, legitimate procreation, and preservation of family in accordance with Islamic law. These purposes are usually reflected in its definition under classical Islamic law and in the current family codes of Muslim-majority countries such as article 4 of the Morocco Family Code 2004, which states that:

> Marriage is a legal contract by which a man and a woman mutually consent to unite in a common and enduring conjugal life. Its purpose is fidelity, virtue and the creation of a stable family, under the supervision of both spouses according to the provisions of this Code.

The marriage contract may be oral or written and it is a binding agreement that creates mutual rights and duties between the couple. A *hadīth* says: 'Fulfil your contracts; and the contract most worthy of fulfilment is that of marriage' (al-Bukhārī), and Q4:21 describes it as a 'firm covenant' (*mīthāq ghalīz*). It is often asked whether the marriage contract is a civil contract under Islamic law or a purely religious sacrament. The legal consequence of that question was explored in the Pakistani case of *Abdul Waheed v Asma Jahangir* [1997], with the court noting that if it was perceived just as any civil contract, then any able adult Muslim woman could contract her own marriage in the same way she could enter into any civil contract, without the consent of a guardian (*waliyy*); but if it was perceived purely as a religious sacrament, then that could imply otherwise.

Based on the *hadīth* that whoever marries has fulfilled half of his religion, the classical jurists considered marriage as partly a devotional act and partly a civil contract. There have been different judicial views on that question in a line of cases. In the earlier case of *Abdul Kadir v Salima Bibi* [1886], the Indian Supreme Court noted that 'marriage according to Mohamedan [i.e. Islamic] law is not a sacrament but a civil contract'. However, in the Pakistani case of *Muhammad Yasin v Khushnuma Khatoon* [1960], the religious nature of marriage in Islam was acknowledged by the court's observation, *inter alia*, that 'there is sanctity attached to it from the beginning to the end by conception of rights and obligations, which, if treated without the holiness which they possess in their nature, would be profane and cease to be Islamic in character'. In the later case of *Kurshid Bibi v Muhamad Amin* [1967], the Pakistani Supreme Court noted that marriage 'among Muslims is not a sacrament, but is in the nature of a civil contract', but acknowledged that '[s]uch a contract undoubtedly has spiritual and moral overtones and undertones, but legally, in essence, it remains a contract between the parties'.

Contextually, 'Abd al 'Atī argues that since every action has religious implications in Islam, it is 'not accurate, therefore, to designate marriage in Islam as either a secular contract or a religious sacrament; it has elements of both'.

Requirements for validity of marriage

There are two main categories of requirements for the validity of an Islamic marriage, namely (i) prerequisites and (ii) essential components of the marriage contract.

The first prerequisite is that both parties to a marriage contract must have legal capacity to do so. Consequently, the legality of child marriages under Islamic law is a topical question of contemporary importance. As the Qur'an does not specify a minimum age of marriage, there are different views on this in classical Islamic jurisprudence, with a majority of jurists allowing child marriages and a minority objecting to it. However, most modern Muslim-majority countries have prohibited or restricted child marriages under their Islamic family law reforms. For example, article 19 of the Morocco Family Code 2004 provides that: 'Men and women acquire the capacity to marry when they are of sound mind and have completed eighteen full Gregorian years of age', with article 20 allowing marriage below 18 years through judicial permission based on legitimate grounds backed by medical evaluation or social enquiry. Similarly, article 10 of the Jordan Personal Status Law 2010 sets the minimum marriage age at 18 years for both parties, but judges may in special circumstances and with the Chief Justice's consent grant permission for marriage of persons aged 15 years.

Second, there must be no legal impediment under Islamic law. The Qur'an prohibits marriage between certain categories of people based on blood relationship, affinity, fosterage, etc. These consist of both permanent and temporary prohibitions that create legal impediments against marriage between parties within those categories. The Islamic legal terminology for these prohibited degrees is *'al-muharramāt'* and the legal authorities for them are Q4:22–4, 2:221 and 2:235, supported by relevant *ahādīth*. Any purported marriage contract within these categories would be null and void *ab initio* under Islamic law. These prohibited degrees have been incorporated into the current legislations of Muslim-majority countries, such as articles 30 and 31 of the Jordan Personal Status Law 2010; articles 56 to 64 of the Morocco Family Code 2004; and sections 9 to 11 of the Malaysian Islamic Family Act 1984.

A third prerequisite under classical Islamic jurisprudence is the requirement of compatibility (*kafāʾah*) between the parties. This requires a woman to be married to a man of equal status to her. Jurisprudentially, there are different views on the scope and constituents of *kafāʾah* as a prerequisite for validity of marriage, with Hanafī jurists being its major protagonists, relying on a *hadīth* which says that women are to be married to men of equal status to them. Other jurists, such as Imām Mālik and Sufyān al-Thawrī, reject *kafāʾah* as a prerequisite for validity of marriage, arguing that there is no evidence that the Prophet or his companions followed this rule in practice.

Although some current legislation, such as articles 21 to 23 of the Jordan Personal Status Law 2010, recognizes the concept of *kafāʾah*, others such as the Morocco Family Code 2004 have abandoned it. Many contemporary scholars challenge the concept on grounds that it has no basis in the Qur'an or the *Sunnah* and that it promotes social stratification, which is not encouraged in Islam. Practically, its force as a prerequisite for validity of marriage has waned considerably in most Muslim societies today.

As for the essential components, classical Islamic jurisprudence prescribes four main pillars (*arkān*) for the validity of a marriage contract, namely: (i) Offer and acceptance, (ii) Marriage guardianship, (iii) Dower (*mahr*), and (iv) Witnesses. The contract may be voidable or void depending on which 'pillar' was absent. There are Qur'anic provisions and *ahādīth* as legal authority for each of the four 'pillars'. They are also minutely discussed in classical *fiqh* manuals, with the jurists expressing different opinions on the substance and scope of each one.

Mutual consent to marriage is expressed through the first pillar, i.e. 'offer' and 'acceptance' between the parties. The classical jurists concur that this is a necessary pillar for a valid marriage contract under Islamic law. The Qur'anic authority often cited for this is

Q2:232—'…do not prevent them from marrying their husbands if they mutually agree between themselves on equitable terms'. Although this verse relates specifically to a revocable divorce, it applies analogically to consent in marriage generally. There are also different *ahādīth* requiring the couple's consent for the validity of a marriage. In one *hadīth*, it is reported that 'A virgin girl came to the Prophet and complained that her father had given her in marriage without her consent and the Prophet gave her the right to repudiate the marriage' (Abū Dāwud).

The 'offer' may proceed from either party followed by 'acceptance' from the other. Both the offer and acceptance may be oral or written. Most current family codes of Muslim-majority countries provide for this pillar as a legal requirement for validity of marriage. For example, article 10(1) of the Morocco Family Code 2004 provides that: 'Marriage is legally concluded by an offer expressed by one of the parties and acceptance by the other, in any accepted expressions from which the meaning of marriage is inferred verbally or conventionally.'

With regard to the second pillar, i.e. marriage guardianship, the classical jurists generally agree that it is a condition of marriage validity to protect the bride's interest. This does not apply to divorcees and widows as they can protect their own interests having experienced previous marriages. This is based on Q2:234—'…when they have completed their waiting periods, there is no blame on you regarding what they do with themselves rightfully'. There are juristic differences in respect of an adult virgin. A majority of jurists considered marriage guardianship as essential for all virgins, relying on Q4:25—'…and marry them with the permission of their people…', as well as a *hadīth* in which the Prophet is reported to have said, 'A woman who marries without a guardian, her marriage is void, void, void' (al-Tirmidhī). Under classical Mālikī jurisprudence the father has an overriding authority (*ijbār*) of marriage guardianship over an adult virgin daughter, which must be exercised in her best interest. Some contemporary Muslim scholars have disputed the validity of this concept of *ijbār*.

However, Hanafī jurists consider that an adult virgin may conclude her own marriage without a marriage guardian, relying also on Q2:234. This Hanafī position has been adopted even by non-Hanafī jurisdictions such as Morocco, with article 25 of the Morocco Family Code 2004 providing that: 'The woman of legal majority may conclude her marriage contract herself or delegate the power to her father or one of her relatives'.

Dower, as the third pillar, is an obligation on the groom and a claimable right of the bride, which she may voluntarily relinquish fully or partly to the husband. This is pursuant to Q4:4—'And give women their dower as a free gift; but if they, of their own pleasure, remit any part of it to you, then consume it with good pleasure.' A *hadīth* also says: 'No marriage is valid except with a guardian, dower and two reliable witnesses' (al-Bayhaqī). Although obligatory, a majority of jurists rely on Q2:236 to hold that the dower is not a legal prerequisite for marriage validity. A marriage contracted without specifying the dower is still valid but the husband would be required to give the wife a suitable or standard dower (*mahr al-mithl*).

The dower can be anything of value under the *shari'ah* as agreed by the couple. The classical jurists concur, based on Q4:20, that there is no maximum limit for it, but differ regarding its minimum. However, a *hadīth* states that 'The best dower is the easiest one' (al-Bayhāqī), which discourages burdensome dowers. Due to demands for exorbitant dowers that hinder young men from marriage, some Muslim-majority countries such as the UAE and Tunisia have, by legislation, set a maximum limit on the dower to ensure social harmony. The agreed dower may be fully paid on the marriage contract or fully deferred to a future date or on demand by the wife. It may also be partly paid on the contract with the balance deferred to a later date.

Having witnesses attesting to the marriage is another pillar of validity of the contract. Secret marriages are invalid under Islamic law. Generally, a minimum of two persons must witness the solemnization of the marriage, based on the *hadīth* that no marriage is valid without two reliable witnesses. The Mālikī and *Shīʿah* jurists opine that the presence of witnesses is recommended but not mandatory for the validity of the marriage contract, provided, according to Mālikī jurists, the marriage is sufficiently publicized. This is based on a *hadīth* in which the Prophet is reported to have said: 'Publicize the marriage, conduct it in the mosque and beat the *daff* drums' (al-Tirmidhī).

Apart from those main requirements, classical *fiqh* manuals of the different jurisprudential schools discuss other subsidiary conditions for the validity of Islamic marriages. One of these is that under *Sunnī* jurisprudence the marriage must be intended to be permanent (*mustadām*). In contrast, *Shīʿah* jurisprudence legitimizes temporary marriages known as *nikāh mutʿah*. According to *Sunnī* jurists, temporary marriages are prohibited, based, *inter alia*, on Q23:5–6—'[The Believers are] those who protect their private parts except with their spouses…'. However, *Shīʿah* jurists justify its permissibility by reference to Q4:24—'… and for the pleasure you derive (*fa mā istamtaʿtum bih*) from them [women], give them their rewards (*ujūr*) as an obligation'. The *Sunnī* jurists further refer to a *hadīth* in which the Prophet is reported to have prohibited temporary marriages during his lifetime, and another report that Caliph ʿUmar confirmed its prohibition, both accounts of which the *Shīʿah* jurists disagree with.

Formalities of the marriage contract

There is no requirement of writing or registration of the marriage contract under classical Islamic law. To solemnize a valid marriage, the officiating minister first certifies that all the requirements for a valid marriage are fulfilled. The couple are then reminded of their marital rights and responsibilities, enjoined to be God-conscious in their relationship, and finally God's blessing is invoked for the couple. However, in pursuance of certainty, oversight, and general welfare (*maslahah*), current legislation in many Muslim-majority countries now requires authorization and registration of Islamic marriages for their validity and recognition by the state. Some examples are articles 65 to 66 of the Morocco Family Code 2004, sections 25 to 34 of the Malaysian Islamic Family Act 1984, and article 36 of the Jordan Personal Status Law 2010.

Effects of a valid marriage

Marriages contracted in accordance with all the legal requirements as analysed above are valid (*saḥīḥ*) according to all jurisprudential schools. Conversely, a marriage that does not fulfil all the requirements may either be void (*bāṭil*) or voidable (*fāsid*) depending on the impeding factor according to the different schools. Current legislation such as section 11 of the Malaysian Islamic Family Act 1984 provides that 'A marriage shall be void unless all conditions necessary, according to [*shari'ah* rules], for the validity thereof are satisfied'. Similarly, article 50 of the Morocco Family Code 2004 provides that: 'When the marriage contract meets all legal requirements, and there are no impediments to the marriage, the marriage is considered a valid one, and leads to the full implication of rights and duties that the Sharia establishes between husband and wife, children and relatives as stated in this [Code].'

A valid Islamic marriage gives rise to specified matrimonial rights and duties, which automatically flow from the conclusion of the marriage contract. The Qur'an generally enjoins upholding familial rights as stated, for example, in Q17:26—'And give the relative their due right…'. The husband's duty to provide maintenance (*nafaqah*) for his wife and children is one of the most important effects of a valid Islamic marriage.

Maintenance (*nafaqah*) in marriage

Maintenance in marriage refers to the financial obligation of a husband towards his wife (and children) during the marriage and during her *'iddah* after a revocable divorce. Under classical Islamic law, a husband is responsible for his wife's basic needs such as feeding, clothing, and lodging on equitable terms or in accordance with their agreement at the time of the marriage contract. This is now reflected in the current legislation of Muslim-majority countries such as article 59(b) of the Jordan Personal Status Law 2010, which provides that: 'The wife's maintenance shall consist of feeding, clothing, lodging, medical care on equitable terms, and a servant for a wife of such a status of being served', and article 189 of the Morocco Family Code 2004, which provides that 'Maintenance shall include food, clothing, medical care, and all that is deemed indispensable, as well as children's education...'. In the case of a revocable divorce, the husband is to sustain the same level of maintenance for the wife during the period of *'iddah* when she continues to live with the husband and is not yet allowed to remarry. Conversely, the wife has a duty to care for the children and the household. She also has to meet the legitimate marital needs of the husband, including conjugal access to her (*tamkīn*) and her loyalty to him (*tā'ah*).

The husband's legal duty to provide maintenance for his wife and children is established by the Qur'an, the *Sunnah*, and *Ijmā'*. Relevant Qur'anic provisions include Q2:233—'Mothers shall breastfeed their children for two whole years for those who desire to complete the suckling term; and the father of the child shall be responsible for their provisions and clothing equitably...', and Q65:6—'Lodge them [during *'iddah*] where you are lodging according to your means, and do not cause them any suffering in order to restrict them...'. There are also many *ahādīth* on the husband's duty to maintain his wife and children. In one *hadīth* the Prophet said: 'They [your wives] have a right over you for their food and clothing according to what is customary' (Muslim).

There is juristic consensus that maintenance is obligatory (*wājib*) on the husband and it is a claimable right of the wife as long as the husband has lawful conjugal access to her. However, the wife is not prohibited from making voluntary contributions to maintenance if she has the means to do so. This is by analogy to Q4:4—'...but if they, of their own pleasure, remit any part of it [their dower] to you, then consume it with good pleasure'. The provision in Q2:233 goes further to state that maintenance must not be a source of humiliation or harm for the wife, rather the husband is expected to discharge the responsibility in a kind manner. There are jurisprudential details on different aspects of the wife's right to maintenance including how it is to be assessed, when it may be forfeited, whether or not a wife can claim unpaid maintenance, and the options available to the wife if the husband defaults or neglects his duty of maintenance.

Lynn Welchman reflects the relevance of the husband's duty of maintenance in most Muslim-majority countries today, by observing that 'The volume of maintenance claims submitted by women to the courts, for themselves and/or their children, testifies to the continuing significance of this obligation, both as part of women's protective strategies and as an economic reality in family life.' Some countries, such as Tunisia, Egypt, and Palestine, have created maintenance funds through which maintenance orders issued by courts are implemented in advance and subsequently recovered from the defaulting husband by the state.

There are detailed provisions on maintenance in the current legislation of Muslim-majority countries such as articles 117–21 of the Afghanistan Civil Code 1977, articles 194–6 of the Morocco Family Code 2004, articles 59 to 71 of the Malaysian Islamic Family Act 1984, and articles 59 to 79 of the Jordan Personal Status Law 2010. Notably, article 40(b) of the Libyan Law No. 10

for Specific Provisions on Marriage and Divorce and their Consequences 1984 provides that 'If the husband is broke and the wife is well-off, she is to provide maintenance for him and her children from him' but article 40(c) provides that 'The wife can ask for divorce if she was not aware of the husband's penury before the marriage'.

The question of polygamy

Polygamy is often ascribed to Islam without qualification, which can be misleading because polygamy is a generic term for either having more than one wife concurrently (polygyny) or having more than one husband concurrently (polyandry). Polyandry is prohibited in Islamic law as stated in Q4:24—'And married women [are prohibited to you in marriage]'. Thus, only polygyny is permissible under classical Islamic law with prescribed conditions. Before the advent of Islam, the pre-Islamic Arabs practised unlimited polygyny and could marry as many wives as they wished concurrently. Islam restricted this through the provision of Q4:3—'…marry women of your choice, two or three or four; but if you fear that you will not be able to deal justly [with them], then [marry] only one…that is more likely to prevent you from injustice'. This is also corroborated by different *ahādīth* limiting the number of wives a Muslim could be married to concurrently to a maximum of four.

Islamic law restricts polygyny to a maximum of four wives concurrently on condition that co-wives must be treated equally justly. Where there is fear of not being able to treat co-wives equally justly, a man should marry only one wife. There are juristic differences on whether the condition to treat co-wives equally is a legal or moral requirement. Incidentally, Q4:129 states that men cannot treat co-wives equally justly, even if they ardently desired to do so, which has led some scholars to argue that this, in effect, enjoins monogamy. That view is, however, critiqued by a majority of Muslim jurists who argue that the Qur'an must not be interpreted to contradict itself, and that Q4:129 referred only to the fact that a man could not necessarily have an equal degree of affection for all his wives in a polygynous marriage. However, there is juristic consensus that polygyny is not obligatory but merely permissible (*mubāh*) under Islamic law. Thus, like any other permissible act under Islamic law, it could be prohibited or restricted if it practically leads to harm or unlawful consequences.

Today, polygyny is regulated in Muslim-majority countries in four main ways: (i) countries such as Saudi Arabia where limited polygyny is legally permissible; (ii) countries such as Tunisia and Turkey where polygyny has been legally prohibited (such prohibition has been criticized by some Muslim jurists as contravening the Qur'anic permissibility of polygyny); (iii) countries such as Jordan, Malaysia, and Pakistan where polygyny is subjected to judicial permission; (iv) situations where a woman may insert a stipulation in her marriage contract entitling her to seek dissolution of her marriage if her husband takes another wife. These situations are currently reflected in the current family codes of different Muslim-majority countries, such as article 59 of the Tunisia Personal Status Law, article 230(1) of the Turkish Criminal Code 2004, article 40 of the Morocco Family Code 2004, article 13 of the Jordan Personal Status Law 2010, and section 23 of the Malaysian Islamic Family Act 1984. In the Malaysian case of *Aishah Abdul Raof v Wan Mohd Yusuf* [1990], the Appeal Committee of the Selangor Syariah Court held that the provisions on judicial permission for polygyny laid out in section 23 of the Malaysian Act were not contrary to Q4:3 but aimed at ensuring that the equality requirement in that verse is respected.

Stipulations in the marriage contract

A wife or husband may insert stipulations in the marriage contract, seeking to protect their respective legitimate rights under Islamic law. This is based on Q5:1—'O you believers, fulfil [all] covenants'. Also a *hadīth* states that: 'Muslims are bound by their stipulations unless it is a condition that permits the prohibited or prohibits the permissible' (al-Tirmidhī). However, both classical and contemporary Islamic jurists differ on the scope of permissible stipulations. For example, in 1995, there were differences of opinion expressed in a debate between the then Rector of al-Azhar University, Shaykh Jād al-Haqq, and the then Grand *Muftī* of Egypt, Dr Muhammad Tantāwī, about the scope of permissible stipulations in an Islamic marriage contract.

Stipulations are classified mainly into valid and invalid stipulations but the issues falling within each category differ amongst the jurisprudential schools. Of the four *Sunnī* schools, the Hanafī is the strictest, the Hanbalī the most lenient, while the Mālikī and Shāfiʿī fall in between with regard to the scope of valid stipulations.

Today the legislations in most Muslim-majority countries are inclined towards Hanbalī jurisprudence for its leniency in respect of valid stipulations. This started with the Ottoman Law of Family Rights of 1917 which allowed stipulations based on Hanbalī *fiqh* and recognized that violation of stipulations by the husband constituted grounds for judicial dissolution of the marriage at the wife's request. The current family codes of most Muslim-majority countries today have comprehensive provisions allowing stipulations in marriage contracts. Examples of such provisions are articles 7, 37, and 38 of the Jordan Personal Status Law 2010 and articles 47 to 49 of the Morocco Family Code 2004.

Dissolution of marriage

Although Islam sanctifies marriage, it also recognizes that circumstances may arise where dissolution of the marriage becomes necessary. Islam does not encourage a couple to stay together in a harmful marriage. This is reflected in Q2:229—'... hold together equitably or separate with kindness...' and Q2:231—'...retain them [wives] equitably or release them equitably; but do not retain them to injure them [or] to take advantage of them. If anyone does that he wrongs his own soul.'

In case of marital discord, Islamic law enjoins attempts at reconciliation before contemplating dissolution of the marriage. This is based on Q4:35—'If you fear a breach between the two [husband and wife], appoint an arbiter from his family and an arbiter from her family; if they both wish for amity, God will effect their reconciliation. God is full of knowledge and is acquainted with all things.'

Many Muslim-majority countries have abolished extra-judicial dissolutions and this reconciliatory process has become part of marriage dissolution proceedings through the courts. For example, article 82 of the Morocco Family Code 2004 provides *inter alia* that 'The court may take all necessary measures, including the appointment of two arbitrators, a family council or whomever it deems qualified to reconcile the couple. In the existence of children, the court undertakes two reconciliation attempts separated by a minimum of 30 days.' Thus, dissolution of marriage is envisaged as a last resort after attempts at reconciliation have failed.

Under classical Islamic law, a marriage may be dissolved either through (i) unilateral dissolution initiated by the husband (*talāq*), (ii) dissolution initiated by the wife (*khul'*), (iii) dissolution by mutual agreement (*mubāra'ah*), or (iv) judicial dissolution (*faskh*).

Unilateral dissolution initiated by the husband (*talāq*)

Talāq is the simplest and most topical method of marriage dissolution. Under classical Islamic law, it can be exercised by the husband at his discretion any time. Although it may be morally wrong or theologically sinful in some circumstances, a husband could legally divorce his wife extra-judicially by the simple statement 'I divorce you', without giving any reason at all. The authority for *talāq* includes Q2:229—'*Talāq* is permitted twice; after that the parties should either hold together equitably or separate with kindness...', Q2:231 and 2:236. Also, a *hadīth* states that 'Every *talāq* is lawful except *talāq* by the imbecile or the insane' (al-Tirmidhī). Jurisprudentially, the rules of *talāq* are classified in relation to form and effects.

Forms of *talāq*

Generally, there are two forms of *talāq*, namely the *sunnah talāq* (*talāq al-sunnah*) and the contra-*sunnah talāq* (*talāq al-bidʿī*). The *sunnah talāq* conforms with the correct process prescribed by the Prophet, while the contra-*sunnah talāq* deviates from that process but, nevertheless, is legally valid according to a majority of jurists. The *sunnah talāq* is further divided into the best type (*talāq ahsan*) and the good type (*talāq hasan*).

The best process for divorcing a wife is through *talāq ahsan*, whereby the husband pronounces a single divorce during the wife's 'period of purity' (*tuhr*), i.e. after her menstrual period and without sexual intercourse with her. The wife's waiting period (*ʿiddah*) then commences for three menstrual cycles. This is based on Q65:1—'O Prophet, when you divorce (*talaqtum*) women, divorce them for their prescribed period and calculate the prescribed period, and be conscious of God, your Lord, and do not turn them out of their homes...'. Also it is reported in a *hadīth* that Ibn ʿUmar divorced his wife while she was menstruating and the Prophet instructed him to take her back and to pronounce the *talāq* when she had completed her menstrual period.

Talāq hasan is the second approved way of unilateral divorce. In this case the husband pronounces three divorces within the *ʿiddah* period, one after each menstrual cycle, without waiting for the woman to complete the required *'iddah* of three menstrual cycles for each pronouncement, but without sexual intercourse with her in between. Through this type of *talāq*, the husband effects an accelerated third and irrevocable divorce. Imām Mālik opines that this is actually a contra-*sunnah talāq* and that only a single pronouncement of divorce is permitted at a time, followed by the prescribed *'iddah* of three menstrual cycles.

The contra-*sunnah talāq* is contrary to the process prescribed by the Prophet. It includes when the husband pronounces the divorce during the wife's menstrual period or pronounces three divorces at once (the so-called 'triple *talāq*') and, according to Imām Mālik, also includes the *talāq hasan*. The jurists of the four *Sunnī* schools generally agree that although this process is theologically wrong and sinful, yet it constitutes a legally valid divorce. The *Shī'ah* jurists however disapprove of this form of divorce and opine that it has no legal validity.

Effects of *talāq*

With regards to its effects, *talāq* is divided into revocable divorce (*talāq rajʿī*) and irrevocable divorce (*talāq bāʾin*). The authority for both is Q2:229—'*Talāq* is permitted twice; after that the parties should either hold together equitably or separate in kindness...'. This means that divorce is only revocable by the husband twice and becomes irrevocable on a third pronouncement.

When the husband pronounces *talāq* on the first and second occasions, the husband may revoke the divorce either expressly or by having sexual relations with the wife during her waiting period. Thus, a revocable divorce does not dissolve the marriage immediately but only suspends it and the wife remains constructively married to the husband until after the prescribed waiting period. Thus, the wife is entitled to full maintenance during the waiting period. If the husband revokes the divorce before completion of the waiting period, there is no need for a new marriage contract as the marriage will automatically resuscitate. If the husband does not revoke the divorce, it transforms into a minor irrevocable divorce (*talāq bā'in baynūnah sughrā*) after the waiting period, and the couple can only reconcile through a new marriage contract. This is based on Q2:228—'Divorced women shall wait concerning themselves for three menstrual cycles; ... and their husbands have better right to take them back in that period if they wish for reconciliation ...'.

The irrevocable divorce separates the wife from the husband and it is divided into minor irrevocable divorce and major irrevocable divorce. The minor irrevocable divorce occurs in different situations, such as when the husband does not revoke a revocable divorce before the end of the wife's *'iddah*, as explained earlier, or he divorces his wife before consummation of the marriage, or the dissolution is obtained by the wife through *khul'*, or by judicial dissolution (*faskh*). The legal consequence is that the marriage is terminated and the couple may only remarry through a new marriage contract without hindrance.

The major irrevocable divorce (*talāq bā'in baynūnah kubrā*) occurs when a third divorce is pronounced by the husband, after exhausting the two revocable opportunities. At this stage the marriage becomes finally terminated and the couple cannot remarry until the woman genuinely marries and consummates a marriage with another man and then gets divorced from the second husband as stipulated in Q2:230—'If a husband divorces his wife [a third time], he cannot remarry her until after she has married another husband and he has divorced her ...'. Upon the coming into effect of an irrevocable divorce, the husband is liable for immediate payment of any deferred dower owed to the wife. If all the dower had been paid, the husband is not entitled to any refund thereof from the wife.

The so-called 'triple *talāq*'

'Triple *talāq*' refers to when the husband pronounces three divorces ('I divorce you, I divorce you, I divorce you' or 'I divorce you three times') in a single spell to the wife. The consequential question is whether this has the effect of a non-revocable third divorce or a single revocable divorce. All the four *Sunnī* jurisprudential schools opine that a triple *talāq* will be legally treated as a third and final irrevocable divorce. Their position is based on a number of *ahādīth* that appear to support that view. For example, Ibn 'Umar was reported to have asked the Prophet whether it was permissible for him to take his wife back after divorcing her thrice and the Prophet said he could not as that would be an act of disobedience. Conversely, individual jurists such as Ibn Taymiyyah, Ibn al-Qayyim al-Jawzīyyah, and some *Shī'ah* jurists as well as most contemporary Islamic jurists consider the triple *talāq* as a single revocable divorce. They also support their position with alternative *ahādīth*. The third position adopted by most *Shī'ah* jurists is that such a divorce is invalid and ineffective because it deviates from the prescribed process of *sunnah talāq*. In the recent case of *Shayara Bano v the Union of India & Others* [2017], the Indian Supreme Court declared the triple *talāq* as unconstitutional in India, and its practice was subsequently criminalized by legislation in 2019.

Contemporary reforms

There have been strong debates in Muslim-majority countries about the abuse of the classical extra-judicial *talāq* and the so-called triple *talāq* by men in ways that have often caused distress to women. Thus, based on the concept of *maslahah* to protect women from men's misuse of their right of *talāq*, many Muslim-majority countries have statutorily prohibited or restricted extra-judicial marriage dissolutions in their current family codes. This has addressed most of the problems and questions about the misuse of the classical right of *talāq* by men today. Although the husband still has the unilateral right of *talāq*, this can only be done through the courts, on whom the duty is conferred of ensuring adherence to due process in accordance with the objectives of the *shari'ah*.

For example, article 78 of the Morocco Family Code 2004 and section 47 of the Malaysian Islamic Family Act 1984 provide that divorce can only be undertaken under judicial supervision, with section 124 of the Malaysian law criminalizing extra-judicial *talāq* with punishment of a fine or imprisonment. Also, article 97 of the Jordan Personal Status Law 2010 provides that 'The husband shall register the divorce of his wife before a judge. If he divorces his wife extra-judicially without registering it, he shall consult the court to register it within one month and anyone who fails to do so shall be liable to the punishment prescribed in the penal code.'

Delegation of the husband's right of *talāq* (*tafwīd al-talāq*)

The husband is permitted to delegate his right of unilateral divorce to a third party, including to his wife, under classical Islamic jurisprudence. For example, both the Shāfi'ī jurisprudential treatise, *'umdah al-sālik*, and the Hanafī jurisprudential treatise, *al-hidāyah*, state explicitly that a husband may delegate his right of *talāq* to a third party including his wife. This is also reflected in current legislation such as article 85 of the Jordan Personal Status Law 2010, which provides that: (a) 'A man may delegate his right of *talāq*, and he may delegate the right to his wife to divorce herself through an official document; (b) If the wife divorces herself through her husband's delegation in accordance with this article such divorce shall be irrevocable.' Today, many women take advantage of this concept known as *tafwīd al-talāq* by negotiating and inserting a stipulation to that effect in the marriage contract to protect their interest in the marriage.

Apart from the husband's unilateral right of *talāq*, there are three alternative methods, namely *khul'* (release), *mubāra'ah* (compromise), or *faskh* (judicial dissolution), through which the wife may also initiate marriage dissolution under Islamic law.

Dissolution initiated by the wife (*khul'*)

Khul' literally means 'to remove' and it technically refers to the wife releasing herself from the marriage by returning the whole or part of the dower to the husband. Where the dower was deferred she forfeits it. There are different jurisprudential views on whether, in settlement for *khul'*, the husband can take more than the dower he gave the wife. Imām Mālik and Imām al-Shāfi'ī held that the husband could take more, while Imām Abū Hanīfah and Imām Ahmad ibn Hanbal were of the view that taking more is disapproved. Other jurists are of the view that it is prohibited for the husband to demand more than the dower he gave, especially if the wife is seeking *khul'* due to cruelty being suffered from the husband. This is based analogically on Q4:20—'If you wish to take a wife in place of another, and you have given the latter a heap of gold [as dower], take nothing back from it; would you take it back based on falsehood and manifest wrong?'

The authority for *khul'* is Q2:229—'...If you fear that they [i.e. husband and wife] will not be able to keep within the limits ordained by God, there is no blame on either of them if she [the wife] gives something to release herself...'. Although the Qur'an does not specifically use the term *khul'*, the concept is inferred from the statement that a woman may give something to release herself from the marriage. A *hadīth* also states that the wife of Thābit ibn Qays came to the Prophet and stated her intention to leave her husband due to her dislike for him. The Prophet then asked her if she was prepared to return the orchard that Thābit gave her as dower and she said 'Yes, and even more' but the Prophet disallowed her from giving more and asked Thābit to accept the orchard and divorce her once (al-Bukhārī). This case is considered as Prophetic precedent for *khul'* and also cited as authority for the unlawfulness of the husband taking back more than the dower he had given the wife.

A majority of the classical jurists agree that *khul'* can be obtained by the wife with or without judicial order, while a minority are of the view that it can only be obtained through judicial order because Thābit's wife brought her petition to the Prophet, who acted as a judge in the situation. Where the husband consents to the wife's *khul'* request, the process can simply be completed extra-judicially, but where he objects to it there are differences of juristic opinion regarding whether the court can impose *khul'* on the husband. A majority of the jurists, including the Hanafīs, Shāfi'īs, and Hanbalīs are of the view that the consent of the husband is necessary, while the Mālikīs hold the view that the court can grant *khul'* to the wife if the husband refuses to consent.

It is submitted that insisting on the husband's consent to *khul'* when it is apparent that the couple cannot continue to live together 'within the limits ordained by God' would endanger the relationship and is contrary to the precedent laid by the Prophet in the petition of Thābit's wife. Two relevant cases in that regard are the Pakistani Supreme Court cases of *Khurshid Bibi v Babu Muhammad Amin* [1967] and *Naseem Akhtar v Muhammad Rafique* [2006] both of which acknowledged that the court has the power to grant *khul'* to the woman where it finds that the parties could not continue to live 'within the limits ordained by God', notwithstanding the husband's objection.

Ibn Rushd in his *bidāyah al-mujtahid* and most contemporary Islamic jurists perceive *khul'* as a no-fault right of marriage dissolution granted to the wife on condition that she pays back the dower to the husband, similar to the right of *talāq* granted to the husband who also forfeits the dower he gave the wife. A majority of the jurists opine that the effect of *khul'* is that of a minor irrevocable divorce.

Similar to *talāq*, the process of *khul'* is also now generally subjected to court procedure in the current family codes of many Muslim-majority countries to ensure due process. Provisions on different aspects of *khul'* are contained in current family codes such as articles 115 to 20 of the Morocco Family Code 2004, articles 102 to 114 of the Jordan Personal Status Law 2010 and section 49 of the Malaysian Islamic Family Act 1984.

Dissolution by mutual agreement (*mubāra'ah*)

Where a couple mutually agree that they can no longer coexist as husband and wife they can dissolve the marriage by mutual agreement known as *mubāra'ah*. It has the effect of a minor irrevocable divorce. Traditionally, this method of marriage dissolution was also effectable extra-judicially, but it is now regulated through a court process in the current family codes of many Muslim-majority countries. For example, article 115 of the Morocco Family Code 2004, provides that:

> The spouses may mutually agree on the principle of ending their conjugal relationship with or without conditions, provided that the conditions do not contradict the provisions of this Code, and do not harm the children's interest. When the spouses agree, one or both of them shall petition the court for divorce, accompanied by the authorization to validate it. The court shall attempt to reconcile the husband and wife. When this proves impossible, the court shall authorize the certification and validation of the divorce.

Judicial dissolution (*faskh*)

On the one hand, a marriage may be annulled by operation of law or by judicial order depending on the circumstances. For example, if it is established that a 'married' couple fall within the prohibited degrees of marriage, their 'marriage' will, upon knowledge of that fact, become annulled automatically by operation of law and the couple can separate without the need for judicial order to that effect. However, either of the parties can seek for a judicial order of annulment if the other party objects to a separation.

On the other hand, judicial dissolution is normally by petition of either party, but usually by the wife, as *talāq* is an easier option for the husband if he does not wish to recover the dower. The wife may bring a petition for judicial dissolution on a variety of legitimate grounds, such as lack of maintenance by the husband; suffering harm, cruelty, or ill-treatment in the marriage; desertion by the husband; or where the husband is suffering from certain diseases such as impotence. In a case of lack of maintenance due to the husband's poverty, there are different jurisprudential views on whether judicial dissolution should be granted. A majority of jurists hold that judicial dissolution can be granted even where the lack of maintenance is due to the husband's poverty. Conversely, the Hanafīs and *Shī'ahs* hold that judicial dissolution is not permissible for lack of maintenance, substantiating their position with Q65:7—'Let the wealthy man spend according to his means, and the man with limited resources spend according to what God has given him; God does not burden any soul more than He has given it.' They argue that this verse recognizes the fact that a man may be rich or poor. They contend that the judge should not grant a dissolution of the marriage if the husband is poor but rather encourage him to find a job to enable him to fulfil his marital responsibilities.

With regard to illness, Imām Mālik declared that the wife can petition for judicial dissolution on grounds of leprosy, insanity, impotence, and contagious skin disease. However, the Mālikī school generally does not limit the grounds of judicial dissolution only to these four diseases. In case of cruelty or ill-treatment, effort will first be made to reconcile the couple through amicable settlement as enjoined in Q4:128—'If a wife fears cruelty or desertion on her husband's part, there is no blame on them if they arrange an amicable settlement between themselves, and such settlement is best.' Where that fails, the wife has a right to seek judicial dissolution through the courts. Such dissolution has the effect of a minor irrevocable divorce.

These different grounds for judicial dissolution are provided for in the current legislation of different Muslim-majority countries. For example, section 52(1) of the Malaysian Islamic Family Act 1984 provides that a woman may seek for judicial dissolution of her marriage on grounds including desertion, lack of maintenance for more than three months, imprisonment of the husband for three years or more, impotency of the husband, insanity, leprosy, and venereal disease, cruelty, etc. Conversely, both article 40 of the Libyan Law No. 10 for Specific Provisions on Marriage and Divorce and their Consequences 1984 and article 109 of the Oman Personal Status Law disallow a well-off wife from seeking dissolution of marriage from a poor husband unless she was not aware of his poverty before the marriage.

After a marriage is validly dissolved under Islamic law, it has a number of consequences. The most significant consequences relate to post-divorce maintenance, consolatory gift for the divorcee, custody (*haḍānah*) and guardianship (*wilāyah*) of children, each of which is comprehensively covered in the classical *fiqh* manuals and current legislation.

Post-divorce maintenance and consolatory gift

Generally, a divorced wife is entitled to maintenance during her waiting period, which may be a duration of three menstrual cycles, three calendar months, or upon delivery of her unborn child, if the divorcee was pregnant. All the jurists agree that the wife's right to maintenance continues during her waiting period after a revocable divorce based on Q65:6—'Lodge them [during *'iddah*] where you are lodging according to your means, and do not cause them any suffering in order to restrict them...'. There are different juristic opinions in the case of irrevocable divorce, with some jurists, including the Hanafis, holding that she would be entitled to full maintenance during that period, while others, including the Hanbalīs, hold that she would be entitled only to lodging during that period, not to other forms of maintenance. A divorcee who is pregnant is, however, entitled to maintenance during her waiting period for either revocable or irrevocable divorce, based on Q65:5—'... if they [divorcees] are pregnant, then spend [in maintenance] on them till the delivery of their pregnancy'. In case of dissolution of marriage through *khul'* the wife is not entitled to maintenance unless she is pregnant, also based on Q65:5. These classical jurisprudential rules have been replicated variably in the current family codes of Muslim-majority countries such as articles 84 and 196 of the Morocco Family Code 2004.

There is also a concept of post-divorce consolatory gift (*mut'ah talāq*), based on Q2:236—'There is no blame on you if you divorce women before consummation or the fixation of their dower; but bestow on them [a suitable gift] (*matti'ū hunna*), the wealthy according to his means and the poor according to his means; a gift of reasonable amount [*matā'an bi al-ma'rūf*] is due from those who wish to do the right thing', Q2:241—'For the divorced women reasonable provision (*matā'un bi al-ma'rūf*) [should be provided] and this is a duty on the righteous', and Q33:49—'O you believers! when you marry believing women and divorce them before you have touched them, then there is no [*'iddah*] period that you should reckon for them. But give them a present [*fa matti'ū hunna*] and release them handsomely.'

The classical jurists held different views on these verses as to which divorcees were entitled to what and whether the post-divorce consolatory gift was obligatory or merely recommended. Today, the current family codes in some Muslim-majority countries make the *mut'ah talāq* obligatory for divorcees in cases where the divorce is determined by the courts to be unfair. For example article 155 of the Jordan Personal Status Law 2010 provides that 'If a husband divorces his wife arbitrarily, such as if he divorces her for no good reason, and she applies to the *qādī*, he shall award her against the man who divorced her such indemnity (*ta'wīd*) not less than the amount of maintenance for one year or more than the amount of maintenance for three years, taking into consideration the circumstances of the husband, whether he is poor or rich. The amount shall be paid in a lump sum if the husband is rich and in instalments if the husband is poor. This shall not affect any of her other rights.' The Jordan law uses the term '*ta'wīd*', which means indemnity or compensation, rather than *mut'ah*. Also article 84 of the Morocco Family Code 2004 provides for payment of *mut'ah* (consolatory gift) as part of the vested rights due to the wife and obligatory on the husband as assessed by the court. Similarly, section 56 of the Malaysian Islamic Family Act 1984 provides that 'In addition to her right to apply for maintenance, a woman who has been divorced without just cause by her husband may apply to the Court for *mut'ah* or a consolatory gift, and the Court may, after hearing the parties and upon being satisfied that the woman has been divorced without just cause, order the husband to pay such sum as may be fair and just according to [*sharī'ah* rulings].'

It is interesting to note that none of these provisions specifically addresses the question of when the wife is wealthier than the husband. This is in view of the fact that under Islamic law a woman owns her own property and could be wealthier than the husband. Jurisprudentially, this will revolve around the question of whether the consolatory gift is prescribed for the divorcee's pain or for her support.

Child custody and guardianship

On dissolution of marriage the mother has a superior right to custody (*haḍānah*) of an infant child, on the presumption that this will serve the best interest of the child, while the father's duty of guardianship (*wilāyah*), including provision of maintenance for the child, subsists after divorce. This is deduced from Q2:233—'Mothers shall suckle their children for two whole years

71

for those who desire to complete the suckling term; and the father of the child shall bear provisions for their feeding and clothing equitably.' There are also many *ahādīth* that serve as authority for the different aspects of *haḍānah*. For example, al-Marghinānī states in his *al-hidāyah* that 'If separation occurs between the parties, then the mother has a superior right to the custody of the child, due to the report that a woman said: "O Prophet! This child of mine, for him my belly is like a cradle, my lap like a tent, and my breast like a beaker, but now his father wants to separate him from me". The Prophet said to her: "You have a superior right to him, as long as you do not marry"…Accordingly there is greater justice in giving the child to the mother.'

It is also reported in another *hadīth* that a woman came to the Prophet and said: 'My husband wants to take away my son, although he [my son] gives me comfort and brings me drinking water from the well.' Her husband contested her claim over the child. The Prophet gave the child an option saying, 'O child, this is your father and this is your mother, make a choice of whomever you want between the two of them.' The son took the hand of the mother and she went away with him (Abū Dāwud).

There is consensus amongst Islamic jurists that the mother has the primary and superior right to the custody of her child, which consists of the duty to physically take care of the child. And the father has the right and duty of guardianship which consists of the right to monitor the child and duty to provide for his maintenance. However, there are differences of juristic opinion regarding the age of the child at which the right to physical custody may revert to the father. Although the mother is listed as having the primary right of custody of the child, the jurists acknowledge, as stated by al-Marghinānī in *al-hidāyah*, that she is not to be forced to undertake custody where it is obvious that she is unable to care for or bring up the child. In such cases, the classical jurisprudential manuals provide rules on the hierarchy of persons entitled to custody in the absence of the mother, most of which prioritize the child's maternal relatives.

Protecting the best interest of the child is the guiding principle on the rules of child custody in Islamic law. Thus, Ibn Qudāmah stated in *al-mughnī* that the principles of custody have been introduced for the welfare of children. Thus, its enforcement shall not be proper in a way that shall put the person and faith of children in jeopardy. Najibah Zin notes that: 'It is a well-established principle that the primary concern in awarding a custody order is the welfare of the child.' Similarly, Mahdi Zahraa and Normi Malek note that 'the protection of the interests of the child is more important than to satisfy the claim of *ahl al-hadanah* [persons entitled to custody]'.

These classical positions on child custody and guardianship have been variably incorporated into the current legislation of Muslim-majority countries such as articles 163 to 172 of the Morocco Family Code 2004 and sections 81 to 86 of the Malaysian Islamic Family Act 1984.

Islamic family law in the West

Islamic family law is habitually applied privately by Muslims living in countries where Islamic law does not formally apply as part of state law. For example, Muslims living in the UK continue to solemnize Islamic marriages (*nikāh*) even though they are not, of their own accord, recognized as legally valid marriages under UK law. Thus, they often complement the *nikāh* with a civil marriage to ensure they have a legally valid marriage under UK law. In the recent case of *Akhter v Khan* [2018], the wife applied to the High Court for a decree of nullity in respect of a *nikāh* solemnized in the UK but not complemented by a civil marriage. The two main questions for determination by the court were: (i) Are the parties to be treated as a validly married couple under

English law by operation of a presumption of marriage? and (ii) If not, is the marriage a void marriage, susceptible to a decree of nullity? In answering these questions, the judge sought to apply what he described as a 'slightly more flexible interpretation' of section 11 of the English Matrimonial Causes Act (MCA) of 1973 to the facts, and held that even though there was no civil marriage ceremony and the *nikāh* did not qualify as an English marriage, the *nikāh* ceremony bore the hallmarks of a marriage even though it was not legally valid under English law, bearing in mind that the parties lived as a married couple for all purposes and that they were treated as validly married in the UAE where they had lived for some time. The court then concluded that the marriage fell within the scope of section 11 of the MCA of 1973 and was a marriage entered into in disregard of certain requirements as to the formation and decided that it was therefore a void marriage (as opposed to a non-marriage) and the wife was entitled to a decree of nullity. This decision was welcomed as a semi-recognition of the *nikāh* as a void rather than a non-marriage under UK law. However, this was short-lived as the High Court decision was overturned by the Court of Appeal in February 2020 in an appeal filed by the Attorney-General's office against the High Court decision.

To ensure that the rights of Muslim women in Islamic marriages in the UK are protected under UK law, a 2018 independent report commissioned by the Home Office recommended amendments to the Marriage Act 1949 and the MCA 1973 to 'ensure that civil marriages are conducted before or at the same time as the Islamic marriage ceremony, bringing Islamic marriage in line with Christian and Jewish marriage in the eyes of the law' in the UK.

Evidently, the continued applicability and practical relevance of Islamic family law both in Muslim-majority countries and in the West cannot be denied. This explains the continued interest in the study of Islamic family law in many Western universities today.

Chapter 5
Law of inheritance

Islamic law of inheritance is a specialized aspect of Islamic family law and its importance is often depicted by reference to a *hadīth* which says: 'Learn [the rules] of inheritance and teach it, for it is half of [all] knowledge' (Ibn Mājah). According to James Anderson '[t]here is no part of Islamic law which is more typical of both the spirit and letter of the Shari'a than is the Islamic law of inheritance'.

Its fundamental rules are prescribed by the Qur'an and the *Sunnah*, giving a list of legal heirs with the aggregate of each heir's entitlement meticulously stated. In the application of the rules, juristic differences however exist in respect of complex cases. But once the relevant jurisprudential rules are well understood it is an immensely logical system.

Origins of the system

In pre-Islamic Arabia, and other parts of the world then, women and children were denied inheritance rights. Inheritance was then based on a custom of agnatization (*ta'ṣīb*), whereby only adult males related to the deceased through an unbroken male line could inherit. Islam reformed that system radically through the revelation of Q4:7—'Men have a share in what the parents and near relatives leave behind, and women have a share in what the parents and near relatives leave behind, out of small or large [property]; an obligatory share.' This was later followed by the revelation of the 'inheritance verses' (Q4:11–12) specifying fixed shares for certain categories of both male and female relatives. Through these verses, the Qur'an reformed the pre-Islamic customary inheritance rules and established a new system that gave male, female, old, and young the right of inheritance under Islamic law. Although *Sunnī* jurisprudence still recognizes a class of agnatic heirs, these have been moved from their traditional position as primary heirs to secondary or residuary heirs after Qur'anic heirs. This is reflected in a *hadīth* which says, 'Give the obligatory shares (*farā'id*) to those entitled to them, and whatever remains is for the closest male agnate' (al-Bukhārī). *Shī'ah* jurisprudence has abandoned the agnatic rules totally.

Two complementary parts

Islamic law of inheritance has two complementary aspects, one obligatory the other optional. The obligatory aspect is based on specific obligatory shares (*farā'id*) allotted to a category of relatives who automatically inherit by operation of law. This aspect creates rules of obligatory 'intestacy' binding on Muslims by operation of law and unalterable. The other aspect represents optional 'testacy' rights through which a person may make a will (*wasiyyah*) bequeathing a limited part of their estate to lawful beneficiaries after death. These two complementary aspects ensure that the closest relatives of the deceased are assured of fixed shares from the estate, while the deceased also has capacity to bequeath some part of the estate to other deserving persons or legitimate causes of their choice. Thus, a Muslim may die either 'partially testate' with a will covering a maximum of one-third of their estate or 'wholly intestate' without a will and the Islamic obligatory intestacy rules apply to the whole of the estate.

The complementary nature of these two aspects of Islamic law of inheritance is well captured by James Anderson as follows:

When the provisions regarding intestate succession are combined
with those relating to testamentary dispositions…the result is a law
of monumental scope and precision, which accords to every
possible claimant an allotment which varies (in most cases)
according to the number of other claimants and their relative
relationship to the deceased, and which ensures that the heirs who
would be entitled on intestacy can never be disinherited by
testamentary disposition, at least unless they themselves consent
thereto, except in so far as one-third of the net estate is concerned.

Writing earlier in 1880, Almaric Rumsey had observed that
Islamic law of inheritance 'comprises, beyond question, the most
refined and elaborate system of rules for the devolution of
property that is known to the civilised world'.

Essential elements

There are three essential elements for the application of Islamic
law of inheritance, namely: (i) the deceased (*muwarrith*), (ii) the
estate (*tarikah*), and (iii) the heir[s] (*wārith[ūn]*).

First, the right of Islamic inheritance arises only after death and
the deceased must be a Muslim. Second, the deceased must have
left behind some lawful assets constituting the estate, which may
include movable and immovable property (*māl*), usufruct
(*manāfiʿ*), or rights and entitlements (*huqūq*), usually classified
into financial rights such as recoverable debts, which are
inheritable, or non-financial rights such as personal titles, which
are not inheritable. Third, the heirs must have survived the
deceased, must be recognized within the law, and not excluded by
any legal bars or rules of inheritance. In case of an unborn child, a
majority of the jurists held that it can only inherit if born alive
after the deceased and its share must be put aside if the estate is
distributed before its birth. The Mālikī view is that distribution of
the estate must be withheld until the birth of any unborn child of
the deceased.

The preliminary rule in Islamic inheritance is that the distribution of the obligatory shares must be from the net estate, after any debts owed by the deceased and/or any lawful bequests have been settled from the estate. This is reflected in Q4:11 and 4:12, each of which contains a specific clause that the legal heirs must take their shares only after settlement of any bequest by the deceased or any debt owed by the deceased. Preliminary deductions would also include burial expenses for the deceased. Some jurists are of the view that burial expenses must be settled first, while others hold that secured debts come first. Thus, even though a testamentary bequest is an optional aspect of Islamic law of inheritance, it must, where the deceased has made one, be settled first before distributing the obligatory shares.

Testamentary bequest (*wasiyyah*)

Chronologically, the rules on testamentary bequest preceded the rules of intestacy under Islamic law. The initial prescription for this was Q2:180, which is known as 'the bequest verse'—'It is prescribed that when death approaches any of you, if he leaves property, that he makes a bequest to parents and next of kin, according to reasonable usage; this is a duty on the God-conscious.' This prescription initially placed a duty of will-making on Muslims before death. However, it is, together with other similar verses such as Q2:240, held to be superseded by later Qur'anic verses which laid down the obligatory intestate rules setting out specific shares for obligatory legal heirs. The jurists hold that an optional right, rather than a duty, of will-making still subsists after the provisions on obligatory intestate rules were revealed. This is based on Q4:11–12, which contain a repetition of the clause that the obligatory legal heirs must take their shares only 'after settlement of any bequests by the deceased or debt'.

While will-making is optional under Islamic law, it is encouraged by the *Sunnah*. A *hadīth* says: 'It is not proper for a Muslim who has got something to bequest, to pass two nights without his written will with him' (al-Bukhārī). Ibn 'Umar is reported to have said that since he heard the Prophet say that, no night passed except that he had his will with him. The optional right of testamentary bequest serves to cater for potential beneficiaries outside the scope of the obligatory legal heirs prescribed by the Qur'an. This could be for individuals other than the obligatory legal heirs or other lawful charitable purposes.

However, a concept of 'necessary bequests' (*wasiyyah wājibah*) has been adopted in Muslim-majority countries such as Egypt, Jordan, Indonesia, and the UAE, whereby certain dependent relatives outside the specified obligatory legal heirs are bequeathed specified shares by law. For example, in Indonesia, the Indonesian Presidential Instruction No. 1 of 1991 on Compilation of Islamic Law accords adopted children specified obligatory bequests under the law. Similarly, in Egypt, orphaned grandchildren are granted specified obligatory bequests from the grandfather's estate, unless the grandfather had already left them a voluntary bequest or gift equal to the obligatory bequest under articles 76–9 of the Egyptian Law of Bequests No. 71 of 1946.

A will may be written or oral, but must be witnessed by two persons, pursuant to Q5:106—'…call to witness between you at the time of will-making, two honest persons…'.

Limitations on testamentary power

There are two main limitations on will-making, which creates a balance between the obligatory and optional aspects of Islamic inheritance law. The first limits the quantum of bequests and is applicable under both *Sunnī* and *Shī'ah* jurisprudence, while the second limits the scope of beneficiaries of bequests according to *Sunnī* jurisprudence.

With regard to quantum, a person may bequeath only up to a maximum of one-third, known as the 'bequeathable third', of the estate by will. This is based on a *hadīth* of Saʿad ibn Abī Waqqās who said: 'The Prophet came to visit me in the year of the farewell pilgrimage when I was severely ill and I said to him: O Prophet, you see how ill I am; I have property and no heir except my daughter. Shall I then give two-thirds of my property as charity? He replied No. I then asked, a half then? He replied No. I then asked, a third? He then replied: A third; and a third is much. It is better that you leave your heirs rich than leaving them destitute begging from neighbours' (al-Bukhārī). All jurists agree that bequests are limited to a maximum of one-third of the estate and bequests that singly or collectively exceed one-third of the testator's estate are void to the extent of the excess. The validity of any excess above the bequeathable third is subject to the consent of all obligatory legal heirs. The Mālikīs hold that the consent of the obligatory legal heirs would transform the excess into a gift from them to the legatee(s). However, if a person does not have any surviving obligatory legal heirs, he may bequeath the whole of his estate by will.

With regard to beneficiaries of a will, *Sunnī* jurisprudence prescribes that a testator cannot make a bequest in favour of any obligatory legal heir as they already have fixed Qur'anic shares. This is also based on a *hadīth* which says 'God has given to each entitled relative their entitlement, so there shall be no bequest for an obligatory legal heir' (Abū Dāwud). According to a majority of jurists, the rationale behind this rule is to prevent interference with the precise balance between the fixed shares of the obligatory legal heirs as prescribed by the Qur'an. However, under *Shīʿah* jurisprudence testamentary bequests may be made in favour of an obligatory legal heir. The *Shīʿah* jurists argue that the 'inheritance verses' only removed the duty of testamentary bequests, not the right to do so, and testators may exercise that right for anyone they wish, including the obligatory legal heirs.

A bequest that satisfies all legal requirements takes effect after the testator's death. Both the obligatory intestacy rules and the optional testamentary rules are sacrosanct under the *sharīʿah* and thus alteration of a lawful Islamic will is prohibited after the deceased, except in case of bequests that are apparently sinful or contrary to public policy under Islamic law. This is pursuant to Q2:181–2—'Whoever alters [a bequest] after hearing it, the guilt shall be on those who alter it…but he who fears an inclination to a wrong course or a sinful act on the part of the testator and effects a correction between the parties, then there is no blame on him…'.

Will-making is therefore lawful and well regulated under Islamic law of inheritance, in its voluntary aspect, based on the Qur'an and the *Sunnah* with concurrence of the Islamic jurists. There are, however, differences of juristic opinion on its different aspects.

Obligatory intestate inheritance and classification of heirs

The obligatory aspect of Islamic inheritance law is based on Qur'anic provisions that allocate specific shares to particular persons as obligatory legal heirs of the deceased. Hanafi jurisprudence classifies heirs into three main specific classes: (i) Qur'anic heirs, (ii) Agnatic heirs, and (iii) Uterine heirs, while *Shīʿah* jurisprudence classifies them generally into heirs by blood relationship (*nasab*) and heirs by marriage (*sabab*).

Qur'anic heirs

The Qur'anic heirs are referred to as *ashāb al-furūd* (possessors of obligatory shares). Under *Sunnī* jurisprudence, they are the heirs who take their respective shares first, followed by nearest surviving agnatic relatives as residuary heirs. The Qur'anic heirs and their respective shares are mentioned in Q4:11, 4:12, and 4:176, with a majority of them being females, which was a radical change to the pre-Islamic rules of inheritance. Basically, nine obligatory Qur'anic heirs (six female and three male) are mentioned in those verses with their specified shares as follows:

1. Pursuant to Q4:12, a **husband** is entitled to ½ of his wife's net estate if the wife dies without a surviving child, and to ¼ if she is survived by a child; and

2. A **wife** is entitled to ¼ of her husband's estate if the husband dies without a surviving child, and to ⅛ if he is survived by a child.

3. Pursuant to Q4:11, a **father** is entitled to ⅙ of his child's net estate if the child dies leaving a child. Where the deceased is survived by only the parents, the father will inherit the remaining ⅔ as the residuary heir after the mother has taken her Qur'anic obligatory share of ⅓; and

4. A **mother** is entitled to ⅙ of her child's net estate if the child dies leaving a child, but she gets ⅓ if the deceased is survived by only the parents and the father inherits the remaining ⅔ as the residuary heir; and

5. A single **daughter** is entitled to ½ of the parent's net estate, when there is no son. If there are two or more daughters they collectively take ⅔ of the net estate. The remainder goes to the agnatic heirs under *Sunnī* jurisprudence, but under *Shī'ah* jurisprudence the remainder goes to the daughter(s) in addition to the Qur'anic shares, giving them the whole of the net estate.

6. Pursuant to Q4:176, a single **full sister** is entitled to ½ of the deceased's net estate, and if there are two or more full sisters they collectively share ⅔, provided the deceased is not survived by a child, father, or brother; and

7. A single **consanguine (paternal) sister** is entitled to ½ of the deceased's net estate, and if there are two or more consanguine sisters they collectively share ⅔ of the deceased's net estate, provided the deceased is not survived by a child, father, full brother, full sister, or consanguine brother.

8. Pursuant to Q4:12, a single **uterine (maternal) brother** is entitled to ⅙ of the deceased's net estate, and if there are two or more uterine brothers they collectively share ⅓ provided the deceased is not survived by a child or father; and

9. A single **uterine (maternal) sister** is entitled to ⅙ of the deceased's net estate, and if there are two or more uterine sisters they collectively share ⅓ provided the deceased is not survived by a child or father.

These nine specific heirs are the only recognized obligatory heirs under *Shī'ah* jurisprudence. *Sunnī* jurisprudence added three alternative obligatory heirs, namely: (i) the paternal grandfather, who takes the share of the father in his absence, (ii) the paternal grandmother who takes the share of the mother in her absence, and (iii) the son's daughter, who takes the share of a daughter in his absence. The first two are based on the *Sunnah* while the third is based on *Ijma'*.

Agnatic heirs

The agnatic heir is the nearest male relative who is connected to the deceased through another male such as a consanguine or full brother. This would also include a son, father, paternal grandfather, paternal uncle, and nephew. The agnatic heirs take any remainders after the Qur'anic heirs have taken their shares.

The male child (Son) is a special agnatic heir. Although he is mentioned in Q4:11, no specific share is allocated to him, rather the provision states that he gets double the share of the female child. Thus, the male child always inherits as a special agnate in his own right (*asabah bi nafsih*) and converts the female child into an 'agnate by another' (*asabah bi ghayrihā*), taking double the share of the female child. He also has the capacity to fully exclude other Qur'anic heirs apart from the husband, wife, father, and mother of the deceased. This can be illustrated by a scenario where a man dies leaving behind a Wife (W), Father (F), Mother (M), Son (Sn), Daughter (D), Brother (B), and Sister (Ss). The distribution of the estate in such a case would be as follows:

W		F		M		Sn		D		B		Ss	
⅛		⅙		⅙		r	(2:1)	r		x		x	
9	+	12	+	12	+	26	+	13	+	0	+	0	= 72

72

In this case, the Wife, pursuant to Q4:12, gets an obligatory share of ⅛ (9/72) as the deceased has surviving children. The Father, pursuant to Q4:11, gets an obligatory share of ⅙ (12/72), and the Mother also, pursuant to Q4:11, gets an obligatory share of ⅙ (12/72). After the Wife, Father, and Mother have taken their obligatory Qur'anic shares, the Son as an 'agnate in his own right' (*asabah bi nafsih*) converts the Daughter into an 'agnate by another' (*asabah bi ghayrihā*) and they together take the remainder (r) fully excluding the Brother and Sister of the deceased from inheritance. The Son, pursuant to Q4:11, shares the remainder (39/72) with the Daughter on a ratio of 2:1, taking 26/72 and the Daughter taking 13/72.

Uterine heirs

The uterine heirs are the third class of heirs after the Qur'anic and agnatic heirs. They are distant kindred who only inherit in default of the Qur'anic and agnatic heirs. They include the daughter's children, the sister's children, the uterine brother's children, the mother's brothers and sisters, amongst others. There is a great deal of jurisprudential difference about the details regarding this class of heirs among the different *Sunnī* schools. For example, traditional Mālikī jurisprudence does not recognize this class of heirs, holding that any remainder of the estate after the Qur'anic and agnatic heirs have taken their shares should go to the state treasury (*bayt al-māl*).

Priorities and exclusions

The rules of priorities and exclusions in Islamic inheritance relate to the degree of proximity between the deceased and the heirs, regarding who has priority in inheritance and who may be excluded. This is based on a systematic hierarchy known as al-Jabarī's rule, named after Imām al-Jabarī, who propounded it. With regard to degree of lineal proximity to the deceased, nearer relatives such as children, parents, husband, and wife take precedence. However, some potential heirs may be fully or partially excluded from inheritance for different reasons identified as legal bars to inheritance. For example, the presence of a child would reduce the shares of the deceased's parents, wife, or husband. This is reflected in the earlier scenario, where the presence of the Son and Daughter reduced the shares of the Father and Mother of the deceased respectively, and, as agnate heirs, fully excluded the Brother and Sister of the deceased from inheritance. Similarly, the presence of a Son totally excludes grandchildren.

A practical illustration

A simple practical illustration could be given of a man who dies leaving behind an estate worth £85,000. His burial expenses cost £5,000, he had a subsisting debt of £25,000, and he left a will of £10,000 for a named orphanage. He was survived by his Wife, Mother, one Son, one Daughter, one Full Brother, and one Full Sister. His estate will be disbursed under Islamic law of inheritance as follows:

The burial expenses of £5,000 and his debt of £25,000 will be settled first. Then the bequest of £10,000 to the orphanage will be settled as it is less than one third of the whole estate and it is for a valid cause. The burial expenses, the debt, and the bequest add up to £40,000. This leaves a net estate of £45,000, which will be distributed amongst the surviving heirs as follows:

- The Wife gets ⅛ of the net estate, pursuant to Q4:12
- The Mother gets ⅙ of the net estate, pursuant to Q4:12
- After the Wife and Mother take their respective shares, the Son and Daughter would share the remainder on a ratio of 2:1 respectively, pursuant to Q4:11
- Based on the rules of exclusion, the Brother and Sister will be excluded from inheritance by the presence of the children.

Thus, the net estate of £45,000 will be shared by the entitled heirs as follows:

• Wife's ⅛	= (9/72)	= £5,625
• Mother's ⅙	= (12/72)	= £7,500
• Son gets 2:1 of remainder	= (34/72)	= £21,250
• Daughter gets 1:2 of remainder	= (17/72)	= £10,625
Total:	= (72/72)	= £45,000

Legal bars to inheritance

Certain acts or attributes create legal bars to inheritance. Traditionally, the main legal grounds for a total bar are: (i) *Homicide*, whereby a murderer is legally barred from inheriting from his victim. This is pursuant to a *hadīth* prohibiting that. (ii) *Illegitimacy*, whereby a child born out of wedlock is legally barred from inheriting from the father under *Sunnī* jurisprudence and barred from inheriting from both the father and mother under *Shī'ah* jurisprudence. (iii) *Difference of religion*, whereby a non-Muslim is legally barred from inheriting from a Muslim and vice versa under *Sunnī* jurisprudence. This is also based on a *hadīth* to that effect. However, under *Shī'ah* jurisprudence, a

Muslim may inherit from a non-Muslim but not vice versa. This legal bar does not extend to wills, except in the case of a murderer.

While these main legal bars to inheritance are generally acknowledged by all jurisprudential schools, there are jurisprudential differences regarding the particular details and circumstances for each of the grounds.

Special cases and doctrines

The complexity of inheritance can give rise to different scenarios not covered specifically by the Qur'anic provisions. Thus, there are jurisprudential rules for addressing scenarios designated as 'special cases' under Islamic inheritance law. These include the cases of intersex individuals and missing persons for which the jurists have established specific rules. Also, when the different fractional shares of respective Qur'anic heirs are added up, they may be equal to a whole number, more than a whole number, or less than a whole number. Where the fractions add up to a whole number that raises no problem, but there are special doctrines for dealing with situations where the specified shares add up to more or less than a whole number. Where the fractions add up to more than a whole number, the doctrine of *'awl* (increase) is applied and the share of each heir in that circumstance will be reduced proportionately, under *Sunnī* jurisprudence. This may be illustrated with the scenario where a deceased is survived only by a Wife (W), Father (F), Mother (M), and two Daughters (2D) as heirs.

W	F	M	2D
⅛	⅙	⅙	⅔
3 +	4 +	4 +	16 = 27

| | | 24 | ↑ (27) |

In this case, the Wife, pursuant to Q4:12, gets an obligatory share of ⅛ (3/24) as the deceased has surviving children. The Father, pursuant to Q4:11, gets an obligatory share of ⅙ (4/24), and the Mother also, pursuant to Q4:11, gets an obligatory share of ⅙ (4/24). The two Daughters, pursuant to Q4:11, collectively get an obligatory share of ⅔ (16/24). These respective shares add up to 27/24, which is more than a whole number. Applying the doctrine of *'awl* the original common denominator of 24 will be 'increased' to 27, which then reduces the respective shares proportionately to 3/27, 4/27, 4/27, and 16/27, adding up to 27/27. This doctrine does not apply under *Shī'ah* jurisprudence, rather, the Wife, Father, and Mother will take their Qur'anic shares of ⅛ (3/24), ⅙ (4/24), ⅙ (4/24), respectively and the two Daughters will inherit as residuaries, sharing the remaining 13/24.

The opposite situation is where the fractions add up to less than a whole number, leaving a residue after all surviving heirs have taken their specified shares without any heir to take the residue. In that situation, the doctrine of *'radd'* (return) is applied and the surplus is proportionally 'returned' to the shares of the surviving heirs. This may be illustrated with the scenario where a deceased is survived by a Daughter (D) and Mother (M) as the only heirs.

D		M	
½		⅙	
3	+	1	= 4
	6		↓ (4)

In this case, the Daughter, pursuant to Q4:11, gets an obligatory share of ½ (3/6) and the mother also, pursuant to Q4:11, gets an obligatory share of ⅙ (1/6). When the two shares are added together it adds up to 4/6, which is less than a whole. Applying the doctrine of '*radd*' the original common denominator of 6 will be reduced to 4, which then increases the respective shares proportionately to ¾ and ¼, adding up to 4/4.

There are many other situations and doctrines apart from these and different jurisprudential views regarding the circumstances and application of the rules relating to different special cases.

The female's share in Islamic inheritance

The rule in Q4:11 and Q4:176 prescribing double the share of the female for the male has attracted criticisms of gender discrimination in Islamic inheritance, especially in contemporary times. This criticism has been challenged by different Muslim scholars. For example, Zainab Chaudhry argues that gender is not the effective cause for this rule of double share, noting that 'it is inaccurate, at the very least, to say that…the females, due to their gender, receive one-half the share of inheritance that male counterparts receive'. She identified different situations where male and female heirs receive equal shares, where female heirs receive double the share of male heirs, where female heirs receive three times the share of male heirs, and where female heirs receive the entire estate respectively. Nevertheless, there is ongoing debate in some Muslim-majority countries advocating full gender equality in inheritance shares in all circumstances. In 2018, the late Tunisian President, Beji Caid Essebsi, placed a draft bill proposing total gender equality in Islamic inheritance before the Tunisian parliament for consideration. The bill attracted mixed responses from within Tunisia and other Muslim-majority countries and seems to have been put in abeyance by the Tunisian parliament.

Under his theory of limits, Muhammad Shahrur has proposed jurisprudentially that the Qur'anic provision on the double share for the male should be understood contextually as not prescribing absolute shares. He argued that 'Islamic inheritance law does not just prescribe one formula for distributing the inheritance but consists of several different options that depend on number, sex, and the nature of the relationship between those who survive the deceased.' With regards to the 2:1 ratio between male and female heirs, he argued that this represents the highest limit for males and lowest limit for females respectively, whereby a male heir's share can never be more than 66.6 per cent but could get lower than that, while a female heir's share can never be lower than 33.3 per cent but could get higher than that. Thus, he argued that if a woman is given 40 per cent and a man 60 per cent or each is given 50 per cent then neither the Upper nor Lower Limit is violated. His proposition has however been contested by many Muslim jurists in view of the specific provisions of Q4:11.

Islamic law of inheritance in the West

Islamic law of inheritance does not apply by default in the West or in other countries where Islamic law does not formally apply. Thus, Muslims living in the West who want their estate to devolve in accordance with Islamic law after their death, would normally effect this by executing a will that fulfils the legal requirements of both Islamic law and the Wills Act of the particular country. Such wills are expertly drafted to incorporate both the obligatory and optional aspects of Islamic inheritance specifying the respective shares of prospective heirs in accordance with the wish of the Testator. In response to growing demand, the Law Society of England and Wales published a practice note in 2014 advising solicitors on how to draft Islamic Wills in conformity with the 1837 Wills Act. The practice note was however withdrawn soon thereafter due to critical secularist feedback that it represented an indirect introduction of Islamic law into UK law.

In most Muslim-majority countries, the rules of Islamic inheritance analysed above are now codified in the current personal status laws, sometimes with necessary modifications.

For example, articles 825 to 948 of the Civil Code of the Islamic Republic of Iran codifies the relevant *Shī'ah* jurisprudential rules of Islamic inheritance, while relevant *Sunnī* jurisprudential rules have been codified in the personal status laws of countries such as Morocco, Egypt, Jordan, and the UAE.

Chapter 6
Law of financial transactions

The growth of the concept of Islamic banking and finance in recent times has increased the relevance of and interest in Islamic law of financial transactions globally. Frank Vogel and Samuel Hayes have observed that Islamic banking and finance has, in the last forty years, 'emerged as one of the most significant and successful modern implementations of the Islamic legal system and a test case for future Islamic legal innovation and development'. It is based on the general rules of contract and commerce as regulated by relevant provisions of the *sharī'ah*. Its fundamental principles are based on the legality of trade but prohibition of usury/interest (*ribā*), predatory/speculative transactions (*gharar*), gambling (*maysir*), and dealing in unlawful goods and services under the *sharī'ah*. Other relevant rules include the principles of partnership and agency, which are employed in devising different '*sharī'ah* -compliant' products in contemporary Islamic banking and finance.

Underlying philosophy and principles

The underlying philosophy of financial transactions in Islamic law is to facilitate distributive justice and equality of opportunities in economic activities. Money is treated as a medium of exchange and not as a commodity in itself. Thus, selling money in the form of a loan with a predetermined interest is prohibited under

Islamic law. Money has a social role to be invested and exposed not only to the possibility of profit but also the risk of loss, similar to other factors of commerce, such as labour. Consequently, the concept of financial transactions under Islamic law is based on equitable profit and loss sharing and not predetermined interest on capital that leaves other factors, such as labour, to bear the risk of loss. This promotes equitable socio-economic justice for everyone involved in economic activities and for society at large.

The principles regulating Islamic law of financial transactions may be grouped into prescribed positive principles that must be observed and proscribed negative principles that must be avoided. The prescribed positive principles are as follows:

1. Encouragement of trade and financial investments.
2. Equitable profit and loss sharing between parties.
3. Sanctity and validity of contracts.
4. Mutual cooperation and social responsibility.
5. Asset-backed financial transactions.

Conversely, the proscribed negative principles are as follows:

1. Prohibition of usury/interest (*ribā*).
2. Prohibition of predatory/speculative transactions (*gharar*).
3. Prohibition of trading in forbidden goods and services, such as alcohol, gambling, and pornography.
4. Prohibition of corruptive or unfair dealings such as hoarding and short-selling.

All of these principles are derived from relevant Qur'anic verses such as Q2:275—'God has made trade permissible and *ribā* forbidden' and Q4:29—'... do not consume your properties among yourselves deceptively, except it be trading by your mutual consent', which are provisions permitting trade and prohibiting *ribā* and other unfair dealings.

Of relevance also are Q5:1—'O you believers, fulfil [all] covenants' and Q2:282—'O you believers, when you deal with one another in transactions involving future obligations for a fixed period of time, write them down...', both of which are provisions relating to validity and sanctity of contracts under Islamic law. Other relevant provisions are Q5:90—'O you believers, intoxicants and gambling...are an abomination and of satan's handiwork, so eschew it so that you may prosper' and Q3:180—'Let not those who hoard the things which God has provided them out of His Grace think it is good for them, nay, it is evil for them', which relate to prohibition of intoxicants, gambling, and hoarding respectively in Islamic commercial transactions.

There are also different *ahādīth* complementing the Qur'anic provisions. For example, a *hadīth* states that: 'The truthful and honest merchant will be in the company of the prophets, the virtuous and martyrs [in the hereafter]' (al-Tirmidhī). Also, when asked which kind of earning is best, the Prophet is reported to have replied: 'Honest trading and a person working with his hands' (Ahmad). In another *hadīth*, he said: 'The buyer and seller have got an option so long as they have not parted. If they speak the truth and disclose [defects] they are blessed in their transactions, and if they conceal [defects] and lie, the blessing in their sale is blotted out' (al-Bukhāri). All these indicate freedom of contract, options in contract, prohibition of deception and predatory commercial transactions.

Other *ahādīth* state that 'He who hoards in order to raise prices is a wrongdoer' (Muslim) and 'Whoever monopolizes in trade is a sinner' (Muslim), which relate to the prohibition of hoarding and monopoly respectively. Also the Prophet is reported to have said 'Don't meet merchandise beforehand till it is taken down to the market' (Muslim) and 'Whoever sells a defective thing without disclosing it continues to be in the wrath of God and the angels continue to curse him' (Ibn Mājah), both of which relate to the prohibition of price manipulation and encouragement of disclosure generally.

Freedom of contract

Generally, there is freedom of contract under Islamic law. Thus, every adult has capacity to contract either by themselves or through agents, while minors can contract through their guardians. This is subject only to legal limitations that amount to illegitimate contracts. The main limitations are the prohibition of *ribā*, *gharar*, and trading in forbidden goods and services under Islamic law. The prohibition of *ribā* and *gharar* is the main distinguishing factor between Islamic and conventional financial transactions. Despite the general consensus (*Ijmāʿ*) on their prohibition, there is some jurisprudential complexity about the legal definition and scope of each of these two concepts.

Juristic analysis of the prohibition of *ribā*

Ribā literally means 'increase' and is specifically prohibited in both the Qur'an and *Sunnah*. There are six specific Qur'anic verses (Q2:275, 2:276. 2:278, 3:130, 4:161, and 30:39) on its prohibition, but there are juristic differences regarding its legal definition and scope, especially in relation to conventional bank interest. Abdullah Saeed notes that there are two predominant juristic views on the definition and scope of *ribā* from the Qur'anic provisions. The first view is that 'any increase charged in a loan transaction over and above the principal [in lieu of deferment, whether stipulated at the time of the contract or imposed subsequently due to payment default] is *riba*' and, by extension, any interest-bearing bank deposits. This view relies on general Qur'anic provisions such as Q2:275 and Q2:278—'O you believers, be God-conscious and relinquish any remnants of *ribā* if you are truly believers.' It is the view supported by a majority of Islamic jurists and is reflected in the Resolution No. 10 (10/2) issued by the Council of the Islamic Fiqh

Academy of the Organization of Islamic Cooperation (OIC) in December 1985, wherein it resolved that:

> Any increase or interest on a debt which has matured, in return for an extension of the maturity date, in case the borrower is unable to pay and the increase (or interest) on the loan at the inception of its agreement, are both forms of usury which is prohibited under Shari'a.

The other view is that the prohibition of *ribā* relates only to 'the exploitation of the economically disadvantaged in the community by the relatively affluent'. This view relies principally on Q3:130—'O you believers, do not consume *ribā*, doubled and multiplied and be conscious of God so that you may be successful', as qualifying the other five verses on *ribā*. Advocates of this view argue that only exorbitant and exploitative interest charged on loans is prohibited. They relate it to the pre-Islamic *ribā* (*ribā al-jāhilyyah*), whereby if a debtor was unable to repay a debt at maturity, the creditor would extend the period by one year and double the debt, and if the debtor could still not pay at the end of one year, it would be doubled again, whereby a debt of 100 could increase to 400 in a couple of years, if not repaid. Jurists who adopt this view perceive *ribā* as not applicable to conventional bank interests. It was in this context that the late Grand Mufti of Egypt, Shaykh Muhammad Tantāwī, issued a *fatwā* in 1989 declaring that 'interest on certain interest-based government investments was not forbidden riba' and later declared that 'interest-bearing bank deposits are perfectly Islamic'. Contemporary Muslim jurists and scholars such as Muhammad Abduh, Rashīd Ridā, Fazlur Rahman, and Muhammad Asad were inclined to this view. However, this view has been critiqued by other Muslim jurists. For example in his explanation of Q3:130 Sayyid Qutb noted that '[s]ome people in our modern times want to manipulate this verse in order to make lawful what God has forbidden. They say that the prohibition is limited only to excessive usury which leads to the multiplication of the principal amount of money time after time.'

Under classical Islamic jurisprudence, *ribā* is classified into two main types. The first is *ribā al-nasī'ah*, which is *ribā* of deferment similar to the pre-Islamic *ribā* and would also, according to a majority of jurists, cover conventional predetermined interest payable on a deferred loan. The second is *ribā al-faḍl*, which is excess paid in on-the-spot transactions of similar commodities. Its prohibition is based on the *Sunnah*, as reflected in the so-called '*hadīth* of six commodities', in which the Prophet is reported to have said: 'Gold in exchange for gold, silver in exchange for silver, wheat in exchange for wheat, barley in exchange for barley, dates in exchange for dates, and salt in exchange for salt; like for like, equal for equal and hand to hand, he who pays extra or asked extra has dealt in *ribā*. The receiver and the giver are equally guilty' (Muslim). This prohibits excess in one of the countervalues in on-the-spot transactions of similar commodities.

Juristic analysis of the prohibition of *gharar*

Gharar is often translated as 'risk', 'uncertainty', or 'speculation', which could be erroneously presumed to prohibit any form of risk or uncertainty in financial transactions. Islamic law acknowledges that every financial transaction involves some element of risk, which is reflected in the theory of profit and loss sharing underlying the whole system. Thus, the concept of *gharar* goes beyond ordinary reasonable risks associated with all business transactions. It is defined as 'the sale of probable items whose existence or characteristics are not certain, the risky nature of which makes the transaction akin to gambling'. Thus the prohibition of *gharar* is linked to the prohibition of gambling in Q5:90. It is also prohibited in the *Sunnah*. A *hadīth* prohibited the sale of an object determined by throwing of a pebble (*hassah*) and *gharar* (Muslim). Other *ahādīth* also prohibited the sale of 'birds in the sky' or 'fish in the sea' before they are caught and the 'unborn calf in its mother's womb'. The prohibition of *gharar* in Islamic financial transactions is meant to prevent people taking undue advantage of others in financial transactions. The jurists often distinguish between major *gharar*, which is prohibited, and minor *gharar*, which refers to reasonable and permissible risk in financial transactions.

Lawful forms of Islamic financial transactions

To avoid the prohibition of *ribā* and *gharar*, Islamic jurists have instituted different forms of '*sharī'ah*-compliant' contracts to facilitate lawful financial transactions under Islamic law. The three main forms are the *murābahah* ('cost-plus' sale), *mushārakah* (equitable partnership), and *mudārabah* (silent partnership). Others include *ijārah* (leasing), *istisnā'* (manufacturing contract), *salam* (advance purchase), and *sukūk* (*sharī'ah*-compliant bonds) amongst others.

Murābahah contract

Murābahah is a contract of sale based on a 'cost-plus' concept. It is a contract whereby a seller agrees with the purchaser to supply a specific commodity on a certain profit added to his cost. The seller must disclose the actual cost he has incurred in sourcing the commodity and the amount of profit he has added to it. The profit may be a lump sum or a percentage of the cost incurred, paid in whole or in instalments by the purchaser. So it is simply a contract of sale agreed on particular terms. Thus, all the Islamic rules of contract and sale apply to it.

Mushārakah contract

Mushārakah is based on joint enterprise or partnership in which partners share both profit and loss equitably according to predetermined ratios often based on the value of investment of each partner on a pro-rata basis. Generally, each of the partners in a *mushārakah* arrangement is entitled to actively participate in the management of the business but the partners may agree that the management would be carried out by any one of them.

Mudārabah contract

A *mudārabah* contract is where one party provides the finance (capital) and the other provides the expertise (labour). The party providing the capital is the *rabb al-māl*, while the party providing the labour is the *mudarrib*. It is like a sleeping partnership, where the owner of capital does not take part in the running of the business. The arrangement of profit sharing is based on agreed ratios with the capital provider often having a larger profit share. On the other hand, any financial loss is completely borne by the capital provider. The capital owner bears the risk of losing money while the *mudarrib* bears the risk of losing the reward of his labour.

Islamic banking products

To be '*sharīʿah*-compliant' all the products and financing modes in Islamic banking must not be contrary to the main principles analysed above. Thus, relevant classical methods of Islamic commercial transactions have been adapted by contemporary Islamic jurists into banking products for both retail and commercial banking and financing in accordance with Islamic law. To ensure *sharīʿah* compliance, the established practice is the constitution of a *Sharīʿah* Supervisory Board (SSB) responsible for ensuring that the products, practices, and all contractual instruments of the bank comply with the *sharīʿah* and with relevant principles of Islamic law. The SSB is also responsible for overseeing the development of new *sharīʿah*-compliant financial products for respective banks from time to time. Normally, the SSB consists of experts in Islamic law of finance. Most Islamic banks in different countries currently have an SSB as part of their

7. **Islamic Bank of Britain in London.**

internal structure. The SSB not only ensures consumer protection, but also helps in securing the Islamic reputation of the bank.

Islamic banking in the West

Today many Islamic banks providing '*sharī'ah*-compliant' financial products are operating side by side with conventional banks in the West. A 2007 policy paper on Islamic finance issued by the Robert Schuman Centre for Advanced Studies of the European University Institute in Italy noted that 'Islamic finance is thriving in Europe, and many major European banks perceive it as a profitable opportunity to generate new business rather than as a threat to existing business.' In the UK, the Financial Services Authority has recognized and supported the Islamic banking initiative within the provisions of the general financial laws and regulations. The system offers an alternative to conventional interest-based banking, and is, incidentally, also patronized by non-Muslims for ethical reasons (see Figure 7).

With the consolidation of Islamic banking globally, there is no doubt that Islamic law of finance has progressed remarkably well in the past forty years, and has even attracted the patronage of non-Muslims for ethical reasons. Despite identified challenges, there are high expectations that it will continue to grow and provide a viable alternative to conventional banking and finance. It must be emphasized that the two sectors are not necessarily a threat to one another and Islamic and conventional banking now coexist harmoniously in different parts of the world including the West. Islamic finance experts argue that a wider adoption of Islamic finance principles can contribute to stemming potential global financial crises of modern times.

Chapter 7
Penal law

In Islamic legal terminology crimes are known generally as *jarā'im* (sing. *jarīmah*) or *jināyāt* (sing. *jināyah*) and their punishments known generally as *'uqūbāt* (sing. *'uqūbah*). Islamic penal law is currently applicable in a few Muslim-majority countries, such as Saudi Arabia, Iran, Pakistan, Brunei, and some states in northern Nigeria. It is the most controversial aspect of Islamic law that often prompts heated debate about its applicability in contemporary times. There are three main academic views about its continued applicability today: (i) that it is an outdated system that must be discarded, (ii) that it is a part of Islamic law that is still applicable, and (iii) that the ideal Islamic polity in which it can be enforced does not exist anywhere today, thus there should be a moratorium against its application until such an ideal polity is realized.

Classical Islamic law classifies crimes and their punishments into three main categories, namely *'hudūd'*, *'qisās'*, and *'ta'zīr'*. Substantively, the *hudūd* and *qisās* offences are specifically prescribed in the Qur'an and/or the *Sunnah*, while the *ta'zīr* offences are left to the discretion of the ruling authority or judges.

Hudūd offences

Hudūd is the plural of *'hadd'*, which literally means 'limit' or 'boundary' and legally refers to specific crimes and punishments set by the *sharīʿah*. Jurisprudentially, the *hudūd* offences and punishments are invariable as long as their constituents are legally proved. Fazlur Rahman has, however, interrogated the term '*hadd*' and its use in classical Islamic jurisprudence for fixed crimes and punishments. He noted that the term '*hudūd*' is used in the Qur'an not with specific reference to crimes and punishments but for the general concept of 'the limits of God' (e.g. Q2:229–30) in theological and moral connotations only. He observes that its use for fixed crimes and punishments was a later jurisprudential development by the classical jurists.

There are six main *hudūd* offences and punishments prescribed under classical Islamic law. They are *sariqah* ('theft'), *hirābah* (brigandage or highway robbery), *zinā* (adultery and fornication), *qadhf* (false accusation of *zinā*), *riddah* (apostasy), and *sharb al-khamr* (drinking intoxicants). The classical jurisprudential interpretations of the substantive *sharīʿah* provisions on each of the *hudūd* offences and their contemporary application have been subjected to critical re-analysis by different contemporary Islamic jurists.

The offence of *sariqah* and its punishment is prescribed in Q5:38–9—'[As for] the male thief and female thief, cut off their hands as a punishment for what they have done, an exemplary punishment from God; and God is Exalted [and]Wise. But whoever repents after his wrong and reforms [himself]; then surely God will turn to him [mercifully]; surely God is Forgiving [and] Merciful.' Ibn Rushd defined this offence as 'taking the property of another by way of stealth, when the thief has not been entrusted with it'.

The classical jurists prescribed two main ingredients for this offence, namely (i) the object must be worth a specified minimum value known as *nisāb* and (ii) the object must have been removed from its customary safe custody (*hirz*) by the thief. Where the definition and the two ingredients are not proved beyond any iota of doubt by the prosecution, the offence of *sariqah* would not be legally established and no punishment of amputation can be imposed. Thus, offences such as breach of trust (*khilsah*), usurpations (*ghasb*), even though punishable as *ta'zīr* offences, do not amount to *sariqah* attracting the *hadd* punishment. Although there is some juristic agreement on the definition of *sariqah*, there are juristic differences regarding the *nisāb* and what amounts to *hirz* in relation to theft. There are also relevant *ahādīth* supplementing the Qur'anic provisions and clarifying the different elements and application of the law on *sariqah*.

Similarly, *hirābah* as a *hadd* offence is based on Q5:33-4—'The punishment for those who wage war against God and His Messenger, and strive to make mischief in the land is that they be executed, or crucified, or have their hands and feet cut off from opposite sides, or exiled from the land; that is a disgrace for them in the world and there is grievous punishment for them in the hereafter. Except those who repent before you have them in your power; so know that God is Forgiving [and] Merciful.'

This offence has been defined as 'waiting by the way (or highway) to steal travellers' property by force and by this obstructing travel on this road'. Its main ingredient relates to the site of the offence. While some jurists are of the view that this offence can only be committed outside a city, others opine that it can also be committed inside a city. The Shāfi'ī school further adds another ingredient, namely, proof of the brigand's strength (*shawkah*) to overpower the victim. There are juristic differences regarding the specifics of both ingredients. There are also juristic differences regarding whether the list of punishments prescribed for this offence in Q5:33 should be applied by gradation or by the discretion of the judge. The minority view is that the judge has a discretion to impose any of the listed punishments, while the majority view is that the listed punishments would be applied by gradation in relation to the severity of harm inflicted on the victim. Thus, where the brigand kills his victim the punishment would be execution, where he only steals his property the punishment would be amputation, and where he caused fear but did not kill the victim or steal property, the punishment would be banishment into exile. Many contemporary scholars such as Kamali argue that the Qur'anic conception of *hirābah* is broad enough to encompass terrorism into its definition.

With regard to *zinā*, Islamic law permits sexual intercourse only between a legally married couple, thus, either adultery or fornication amounts to the offence of *zinā*. The provision for this offence and its punishment is based on Q24:2—'[As for] the woman and the man guilty of *zinā*, flog each of them with a hundred lashes; let no compassion move you in their case, in a matter prescribed by God if you believe in God and the last day, and let a party of believers witness their punishment.' Mohammad Salim El-Awa defines it as 'all sexual intercourse between a man and a woman without legal right or without the semblance of legal right'. The concept of 'semblance of legal right' (*shubhah*) leaves room for juristic disagreement. Thus, in his *bidāyah al-mujtahid*, Ibn Rushd identified that the jurists differ about what is meant by semblance (*shubhah*) of marriage. The main ingredient for this offence is actual penetrative intercourse between a man and a woman outside a legitimate marriage relationship. In proving this offence, all the four required witnesses must testify that they saw the couple physically in this condition.

While all classical jurists agree that *zinā* covers both fornication and adultery, the punishment of a hundred lashes prescribed in Q24:2 is applied only to fornication, while, based on the *Sunnah*, the punishment prescribed for adultery is stoning to death (*rajm*). This is based on a *hadīth* stating that the punishment for adultery by a married person was stoning. However, while there is agreement amongst the main Islamic jurisprudential schools on the punishment of stoning for adultery based on the *Sunnah*, the *Mu'tazilah* sect opposed the punishment of stoning on grounds that it has no existing Qur'anic authority. In 1981, the punishment of stoning for adultery was challenged as being un-Islamic in the Pakistani Federal Shariat Court in the case of *Hazoor Bukhsh v Federation of Pakistan* [1981]. The court initially ruled by a majority decision of four to one that the punishment of stoning was repugnant to Islam and that such punishment cannot be specifically found in the Qur'an. However, due to protests instigated by traditional clerics against the court's decision, the state was forced to appeal for a review of the decision by a reconstituted bench of the court. The reconstituted court reviewed the earlier decision and declared in *Federation of Pakistan v Hazoor Bukhsh and Others* [1982] that even though the punishment of stoning is not found in the Qur'an, there was authority for it in the *Sunnah* and thus the punishment was lawful under Islamic law. The punishment of stoning for adultery has, however, never been awarded in Pakistan due to the strict evidential requirements for the offence. The punishment of stoning for adultery continues to be contentious amongst contemporary Islamic scholars.

To be punished for *zinā,* the unlawful intercourse must have been committed wilfully. Thus, modern Islamic penal codes, such as section 4 of the Pakistan Offence of Zina (Enforcement of Hudood) Ordinance, 1979 and section 68(1) of the Brunei Syariah Penal Code, 2013, define *zinā* as *wilful sexual intercourse* between a man and woman who are not legally married to each other. This therefore excludes victims of rape from being punishable for *zinā* as they have not submitted wilfully to the unlawful sexual intercourse. Kamali notes that '[M]uslim jurists are in agreement to the effect that a woman who has been raped and subjected to irresistible force is not liable to any punishment', based on the *hadīth* in which the Prophet said: 'Certainly, God has pardoned my community for mistake, forgetfulness or things they are forced to do under duress' (Ibn Mājah). Rape *(ightisāb)* is itself recognized as a heinous crime under classical Islamic law and the offender is punishable for it. Some of the classical Muslim jurists classified rape as an offence punishable under *zinā*, while others classified it as an offence punishable under *hirābah*, as they perceived it, respectively, as having ingredients of either of these two *hudūd* offences. Modern Islamic penal codes, such as the Shari'ah Penal Code Law of Zamfara State of Nigeria 2000, also criminalize rape, defining it as having unlawful sexual intercourse with someone by coercion or without the victim's consent.

Due to the severe punishment for *zinā*, an accusation of the offence without required proof constitutes the offence of *qadhf* (false accusation of *zinā*). This is provided for in Q24:4–5—'And those who accuse chaste women and produce not four witnesses, flog them with eighty lashes and reject their evidence ever after, for they are wicked transgressors. Except those who repent thereafter and act aright; for surely God is Forgiving [and] Merciful.'

El-Awa defines *qadhf* as 'unproved allegation that an individual has committed *zinā*'. However, there is disagreement amongst the Islamic jurists as to whether or not the accusation must be precise or could be implied. While a majority of the jurists hold that only precise unproven allegations of *zinā* could amount to *qadhf*, the Mālikī jurists are of the view that implied allegations may also establish the offence. This offence serves essentially as a deterrent against careless accusations of *zinā* due to the difficulty in proving the latter, to the extent that if three witnesses corroborate the evidences of one another but not the fourth, all the witnesses will be guilty of *qadhf* and liable to the prescribed punishment of eighty lashes for unproved allegation of *zinā*.

Also all the classical jurisprudential schools list apostasy as a *hadd* offence punishable by death. Apostasy can be committed by a Muslim either by denouncing Islam expressly or by implication, by, for example, desecrating the Qur'an. Under classical jurisprudence the apostate is given three days to repent or otherwise would be executed. The Hanafīs exempt women apostates from this punishment. However, the definition of apostasy has been contentious about whether apostasy *simpliciter*, i.e. bare change of religion by an individual, is a *hadd* offence punishable by death. While Qur'anic provisions such as Q2:217, 3:90, 4:137, and 47:25 denounce apostasizing from Islam, there is no prescribed punishment for it in the Qur'an. Also, Q2:256 states clearly that: 'There is no compulsion in religion; certainly guidance is clear from misguidance.' Thus, many contemporary Muslim jurists argue that apostasy *simpliciter* is not a *hadd* offence punishable with death, except when it involves acts of treason against the state. El-Awa argues that declaring change of religion by an individual as apostasy punishable by death is contrary to the clear Qur'anic declaration of no compulsion in religion. Some classical jurists had also differed on this since the early period of Islam. For example, the Hanbalī jurist Ibn Taymiyyah stated that some successors to the Prophet's companions, known as *al-tābi'ūn*, such as Ibrahim al-Nakha'ī (d. 718 CE) and Sufyān al-Thawrī (d. 884 CE), who were both leading Islamic jurists of their time, held the view that a Muslim apostate must never be sentenced to death but should by all means be invited back to Islam.

Both El-Awa and Kamali make references to the Qur'an, the *Sunnah*, and different juristic views to argue that apostasy *simpliciter* neither constitutes a *hadd* offence nor attracts the death penalty. They cited the 12th-century Mālikī jurist Abū al-Walīd al-Bājī as stating that apostasy *simpliciter* was a sin for which there is no *hadd* punishment. In his *Muslim Conduct of State*, Muhammad Hamidullah also argued that the punishment of apostasy is linked to treason against the state because '[t]he basis of Muslim polity being religious…, it is not difficult to appreciate the reason for penalizing this act of apostasy [f]or it constitutes a politico-religious rebellion'.

The death penalty for apostasy was based on two main traditions of the Prophet. The first *hadīth* says: 'Anyone who changes his religion, kill him' (al-Bukhārī). Some jurists identify it as a solitary (*ahhād*) *hadīth*, which cannot sustain a death penalty, while others identify weakness in its transmission and thus challenge its general legal value. The second *hadīth* says: 'It is illegal to spill the blood of a Muslim except in one of three cases: the adulterer/adulteress, a life for a life and one who forsakes his religion and separates from the community' (al-Bukhārī). Contemporary jurists argue that it is clear from this *hadīth* that 'one who forsakes his religion and separates from the community' refers to the offence of treason rather than apostasy *simpliciter*. S. A. Rahman argued that although there were incidents of apostasy during the Prophet's time, there is no record of the Prophet sentencing anyone to death for apostasy *simpliciter*. Thus, El-Awa concluded that the Qur'an does not prescribe a worldly punishment for apostasy and the Prophet never implemented such punishment, but some companions of the Prophet recognized it as a sin subject to *ta'zīr* (discretionary) punishment.

Drinking of intoxicants is also a *hadd* offence under all the main classical jurisprudential schools. Qur'anic revelation towards its prohibition came in three stages, first a warning about it in Q2:219—'They ask you about intoxicants and gambling, say: "in both of them is great sin and some benefit for people, but the sin in both of them is greater than their benefit"...', then a restriction on it in Q4:43—'O you believers, do not approach the prayer when you are intoxicated until you know well what you say...', and finally its full prohibition in Q5:90—'O you believers, intoxicants and gambling and idolatry and divination are an abomination; from the handiwork of satan, so abstain from it so that you may prosper.' Different *ahādīth* also corroborate this prohibition. While there is juristic consensus on its prohibition, the Qur'an does not prescribe a punishment for it. However, the Prophet is reported in different *ahādīth* to have penalized the drunk by beating them with different objects such as date-palm fronds and sandals. It is recorded that Caliph Abū Bakr penalized drunkenness with forty whip lashes and Caliph 'Umar increased it to eighty whip lashes due to the high rate of drunkenness during his time. A majority of the jurists prescribe eighty lashes while a minority prescribe forty lashes for this offence. Thus, some contemporary scholars such as El-Awa contend that this reflects a *ta'zīr* offence because of the differences about its exact punishment, which does not satisfy the fixed nature of *hudūd* punishments.

Repentance as a mitigating factor for *hudūd* punishments

It is noteworthy that most of the respective Qur'anic prescriptions for the *hudūd* offences are followed immediately by what may be called a 'repentance clause'. For example, the prescription on *sariqah* in Q5:38 is immediately followed by a proviso in Q5:39—'But whoever repents after his wrong and reforms, then surely God will forgive him, surely God is Forgiving [and] Merciful.' Similar clauses are found in Q5:34 for *hirābah* and in Q24:5 for *qadhf* offences.

All the four *Sunnī* jurisprudential schools concur that repentance serves as full mitigation against the punishment for apostasy. Normally the apostate is allowed time to repent and if he repents then the punishment is waived. Also there is agreement that in the case of *hirābah*, repentance before the bandit is apprehended is a mitigating factor for waiving the *hadd* punishment. This is based on the clear statement in Q5:34—'Except for those who repent before they fall into your power...'. The jurists differ on the scope of extending this rule to the other *hudūd* offences. Notably, a *hadīth* says: 'Pardon the *hudūd* amongst yourselves, for when a *hadd* offence is reported to me it becomes obligatory' (Abū Dāwud).

Apart from the six *hudūd* offences mentioned above, some jurists add a seventh *hadd* offence, namely rebellion (*baghy*) based on Q49:9, while others consider it as a political offence that is dealt

with by the political authority under the doctrine of *siyāsah*.
Different Islamic jurisprudential manuals, such as Volume 2 of
Nyazee's English translation of Ibn Rushd's *bidāyah al-mujtahid*,
give further details on the different jurisprudential opinions on
relevant issues relating to each of the *hudūd* offences.

Qisās offences

Qisās literally means 'equal retaliation' and legally it refers to
offences of homicide and bodily injuries that attract retributive
punishments under Islamic law. This category of offences is based
on the concept of *lex talionis* as prescribed in Q2:178—'O you
believers, *qisās* is prescribed for you in cases of homicide…but if
any remission is made by the kin of the slain, then comply
reasonably, and compensate him with gratitude; that is a
concession and a mercy from your Lord…'. Also Q5:45 states—'We
ordained therein [in the Torah] for them that: life for life, eye for
eye, nose for nose, ear for ear, tooth for tooth, and wounds by
equal retaliation. But if anyone remits the retaliation by way of
charity it will be an act of atonement for him…'. However, some
jurists argue that Q5:45 refers to the Jewish prescription in the
Torah, and that *qisās* for bodily injuries under Islamic law is based
on *Ijmā*', not on this verse.

Where proved, four options of punishments are prescribed for
qisās offences, namely (i) equal retaliation for homicide or injury
(*qisās*), (ii) payment of compensation often called 'blood money'
(*diyah*), (iii) atonement (*kaffārah*), and (iv) complete pardon (*afw*).
The choice amongst these four options depends on the discretion
of the heirs of the deceased in case of homicide and the discretion
of the victim in the case of bodily injuries. Due to the role of the
victim or the heirs in deciding which punishment applies in *qisās*
cases, this category of offences has a dual nature of a crime and a
tort. The Mālikī school holds that where the heirs of the deceased
in homicide cases or the victim of bodily injuries opts for

compensation or pardon instead of actual retaliation, the state should still impose a *taʿzīr* punishment to serve as a deterrent from crimes. Thus, El-Awa asserts that *qisās* offences 'have a dual nature, that of a crime for which punishment is imposed [by the state] and that of a tort which makes the wrongdoer liable to pay a compensation from which the wronged may benefit'.

Taʿzīr offences

Legally, *taʿzīr* refers to all other offences other than *hudūd* and *qisās* under Islamic law. This covers all offences not specifically mentioned in the Qur'an and/or the *Sunnah* or for which no specific punishment has been prescribed in either the Qur'an or the *Sunnah*. The main characteristic of *taʿzīr* is that it emanates from the discretion of the state as delegated to the judge. The authority for *taʿzīr* is often based on Q4:16—'And as for the two who are guilty of indecency among you, punish them both.'

The discretion for *taʿzīr* is in relation to both the determination of the offence and the prescription of its punishment, as long as the offence is not otherwise permissible under the *sharīʿah* and the punishment prescribed not otherwise prohibited under the *sharīʿah*. Through *taʿzīr*, the state is conferred with the discretion to regulate and punish conduct that is contrary to social harmony and public security within the general scope of the *sharīʿah*. Contemporary heinous offences such as terrorism and suicide bombing would also come under *taʿzīr* offences for scholars who do not classify them under *hudūd* offences.

Evidential requirements and standard of proving criminal offences

All *hudūd* crimes must be proved beyond any iota of doubt under Islamic law. The evidential requirements in *taʿzīr* offences are slightly less stringent than in *hudūd* offences, according to the different jurisprudential schools. A *hadīth* prescribes that the *hudūd* punishments must be averted in case of any iota of doubt. Under Islamic criminal justice the onus of establishing the ingredients and proving the offence is on the prosecution and where it fails to do so or where the accused person is able to create any iota of doubt in that regard, then the *hadd* punishment must be averted. Apart from *zinā*, which requires four corroborating witnesses, all other criminal offences require the testimony of two witnesses or confession by the offender.

The classical Islamic penal rules are now codified into the current penal codes of a few Muslim-majority countries, with necessary modifications. Recently, Brunei adopted a new *Syariah* Penal Code Order 2013 codifying the classical categorization of crimes and punishments. Article 52 of the code defines *hadd* as 'punishment or penalty as ordained by the Al-Qur'an or Sunnah...for the offences of *sariqah*, *hirabah*, *zina*, *qazaf*, drinking intoxicating drinks and *irtidad*'.

Human rights concerns

Today, the application of Islamic penal law has continued to attract human rights concerns in respect of the prescribed punishments such as amputation, crucifixion, stoning, and flogging, which are considered by human rights advocates as being violative of the international prohibition of torture or cruel, inhuman, or degrading treatment or punishment under human rights law. In addressing the human rights concerns, Mashood Baderin has argued the need for adequate legal representation in the *sharī'ah* courts to ensure that fair trial and due process are maintained in the criminal justice systems of relevant Muslim-majority countries. In Muhammad Shahrur's view, the prescribed *hudūd* punishments should be understood as representing the upper limits of punishment for the respective offences, and the state could legitimately apply lesser punishments below those upper limits. It is insightful to conclude this chapter with Kamali's observation that:

Muslim countries and jurisdictions have generally shied away from the enforcement of *hudūd* punishments due to their apparent severity. Yet because of public sensitivities and politicisation of the subject, parliamentarians, judges, and jurists have also not shown a willingness to depart from hallowed precedents in favour of a fresh and holistic understanding of Qur'anic dispensations of *hudūd*. This naturally makes the challenge of adjustment and reform even more difficult.

Chapter 8
International law (*al-siyar*)

Islamic international law is known as '*al-siyar*' and Muhammad al-Shaybānī (749/50–805 CE), who is acknowledged as the most prolific classical jurist on the subject, is perceived as the Hugo Grotius of the Muslims. The former ICJ judge, Christopher Weeramantry, identified al-Shaybānī as the author of the most detailed early treatise on international law and observed that *al-siyar* was a precursor for the development of contemporary international law. Al-Shaybānī's writings continue to influence Islamic legal thinking on international law even in contemporary times. He devoted two books exclusively to the subject of Islamic international law, namely *kitāb al-siyar al-saghīr* (The Shorter Book on International Law) and *kitāb al-siyar al-kabīr* (The Longer Book on International Law). Both were written in the 8th century.

Al-siyar covers the classical Islamic rules on state conduct in times of war and peace such as treaty rules, territorial jurisdiction, rules of warfare, and diplomatic relations, etc. Exploring the relationship between the classical principles of *al-siyar* and contemporary international law has become a subject of increasing academic research in recent times. While some contemporary international law jurists, such as Weeramantry, see a general compatibility between *al-siyar* and contemporary international law, others, such as Anke Bousenita, view the two

systems as incompatible. Writing in 1962, the former Vice
President and General Counsel of the World Bank, the late
Ibrahim Shihata, argued the need for understanding Islamic
international law 'to verify the extent of its past contributions to
the development of [contemporary] international law, and to
survey the possibilities of its further contributions in the future' to
ensure that contemporary international law becomes 'a more
readily accepted system to...the Muslim world'.

Scope of Islamic international law

The rules of Islamic international law are derived from the
Qur'an, the *Sunnah*, and relevant practices of the earliest Muslim
caliphs. Its classical rules cover most of the relevant issues in
contemporary international law, some of which are briefly
analysed below.

Islamic law of treaties

Treaties are known as *mu'āhadāt* under Islamic international law
and, being the major means for regulating state relationships,
their importance is well acknowledged both in theory and
practice. It was noted in Chapter 2 that an important legislative
step taken by Prophet Muhammad when he arrived in Madīnah
was the adoption of the 'Charter of Madīnah' to regulate the
relationship between the Muslims and other residents of Madīnah
at the time. Another example is the 'Treaty of Hudaybiyyah'
negotiated in 625 CE between the Prophet on behalf of the
Muslims and Suhayl ibn 'Amr on behalf of the Makkans to agree a
ten-year peace pact between them. Based on the treaty of
Hudaybiyyah, some scholars, such as Khadduri, relying on the
opinion of the Shāfi'ī school, argued that Islamic international law
only allows for a peace treaty for a period not exceeding ten years.
That view is contestable, as both the Hanbalī jurist Ibn Qudāmah
and the Mālikī jurist Ibn Rushd explain that there are other
opinions, such as that of Abū Hanīfah, to the effect that there can

be peace treaties for unlimited periods between Muslims and non-Muslims.

The principle that treaties must be fulfilled in good faith (*pacta sunt servanda*) is well acknowledged under Islamic international law pursuant to Q5:1—'O you believers, fulfil [all] covenants.' This was confirmed in the case of *Saudi Arabia v Aramco* [1963], wherein the tribunal referred to Q5:1 to acknowledge the importance of compliance with treaty obligations under Islamic law. Equality in treaty relations is also recognized under Q8:58— 'If you fear treachery from a people [with whom you have entered a treaty], throw out [their treaty] to them to place you on equal terms; for God does not love the treacherous.' The Prophet corroborated this in a *hadīth* that 'Whoever has a treaty of peace with a people should not loosen or tighten it [beyond its terms] until the treaty reaches its appointed term. Otherwise, he should declare the treaty null and void so that they are both on equal terms' (Abū Dāwud).

Based on the injunction in Q2:282—'O you believers, when you contract a debt for a fixed time, put it in writing…' and the practices of the Prophet, al-Shaybānī and other classical Islamic jurists noted that a treaty must be in writing and indicate its date of adoption, date of entering into force, and its duration. It is also acknowledged that there is no limit to the subject matter of treaties under Islamic international law. While there is general juristic consensus on fulfilling treaty obligations, there are different juristic views regarding some of the rules on treaties, which are analysed in the classical *fiqh* manuals and by contemporary writers on the subject.

Islamic law of armed conflict

Regulating the use of force is one of the most problematic aspects of international law. This relates to the legality of warfare, *jus ad bellum*. Under contemporary international law, article 2(4) of the

UN Charter prohibits aggressive use of force, except in cases of self-defence pursuant to article 51 of the UN Charter, and collective security authorized under article 42 by the UN Security Council. The Islamic concept of *jihād* is often misrepresented as aggressive warfare that violates the regulation of use of force under contemporary international law.

Based on out-of-context references to Qur'anic provisions and classical juristic views, a minority of commentators and so-called 'Islamist' militant groups advocate a concept of 'offensive *jihād*' under Islamic international law. Such perception of *jihād* is clearly violative of the prohibition of aggressive use of force under both *al-siyar* and contemporary international law. The concept of *jihād* must be understood in the context of its evolution from the 7th century through different periods of Islamic history up to the present time. Similar to the evolution of the concept of warfare over time, the overwhelming majority of Islamic jurists acknowledge that the concept of *jihād* today excludes the notion of an offensive *jihād*. Said Mahmoudi has noted that '[w]hen *jihād* is invoked by resistance or militant groups to justify attacks, there is reason to be hesitant about accepting this as sanctioned by Islam'.

The majority juristic position is that aggressive use of force is prohibited under *al-siyar*. Long before the adoption of the UN Charter, classical rules of *al-siyar* permitted the use of force only in self-defence and collective measures. This is based on specific Qur'anic provisions and traditions of the Prophet. The general rule on warfare under Islamic international law is contained in Q2:190—'And fight in the path of God those who fight you, but do not transgress; certainly God does not love those who transgress.' Chronologically, the first permission given to Muslims for the use of force was with reference to self-defence in Q22:39—'Permission [to fight] is given to those upon whom war is made because they have been wronged; and certainly God is well able to assist them.' This gave permission to the Prophet and the Muslims who had taken refuge in Madīnah to fight back against their enemies who continued to harass them in different ways. These two Qur'anic verses clearly exclude aggressive or transgressive use of force. The justification for use of force in self-defence is provided in Q9:13–'Will you not fight against a people who broke their oaths [of peace] and aimed at expelling the Prophet and attacked you first?' This is corroborated by a *hadīth* which states that whoever is killed fighting in defence of his property, family, himself, or his religion, dies as a martyr (Abū Dāwud). The use of force for collective measures is also acknowledged in Q49:10, which is similar to the concept of collective security under contemporary international law, as a means for dealing with apparent threats to peace and security under Islamic law.

The possible use of force for humanitarian purposes is also acknowledged in Q4:75–'And why should you not fight in the cause of God and of those who being weak are ill-treated and oppressed; men, women and children whose cry is: "Our Lord!, rescue us from this land whose people are oppressors; and raise for us by Your grace one who will protect; and raise for us by Your grace one who will help."' Sohail Hashmi argues, based on this Qur'anic verse, that 'the ethics of humanitarian intervention in Islam must be seen as a subset of the general theory of *jihad*' for humanitarian purposes.

Islamic humanitarian law

The rules of humanitarian law regulate conduct in warfare, *jus in bello*, to ensure that warfare is conducted according to defined humanitarian principles. Such rules are an important component of the law of war under classical *al-siyar* rules. Similar to contemporary international law, there are more rules relating to *jus in bello* than to *jus ad bellum* under Islamic laws of war.

Islamic law had recognized the need for constraint in warfare as early as Prophet Muhammad's time, as evidenced by his consistent orders to the Muslim army urging restraint and humanitarianism in war. Cheriff Bassiouni has noted that these early instructions of the Prophet later formed the basis of the traditional rules of armed conflict under Islamic international law 'codified in the eighth century CE by al-Shaybāni (d. 189 AH/804 CE) in his famous book *al-Siyar* [which] ... constituted the most developed articulation of IHL until the twentieth century CE, when the foundations of modern customary and conventional international humanitarian laws were laid'. Similar to contemporary international humanitarian law, Islamic law prohibits mutilations, unnecessary destructions, unnecessary bloodshed, unnecessary human suffering, and all excesses in warfare. The general tone for constraint in warfare under Islamic law is set in Q2:190, which clearly indicates that there are limits in warfare that should not be exceeded under Islamic law. The details of these limits are found in the recorded traditions of the Prophet and the practices of the orthodox caliphs after him. It is recorded that during his lifetime, whenever Prophet Muhammad appointed a commander for warfare, he enjoined him with God-consciousness and gave orders for restraint in warfare as follows:

> ... never commit breach of trust nor treachery nor mutilate anybody
> nor kill any minor or woman. This is the pact of God and the
> conduct of His Messenger for your guidance .... In avenging the
> injuries inflicted upon us molest not the harmless inmates of
> domestic seclusion; spare the weakness of the female sex; injure not
> the infants at the breast or those who are ill in bed. Refrain from
> demolishing the houses of unresisting inhabitants; destroy not the
> means of subsistence, nor their fruit-trees and touch not the
> palm ... and do not kill children.

This practice was sustained by the four orthodox caliphs and by subsequent Muslim rulers after them. It is reported that the first caliph, Abu Bakr, would also order the Muslim army as follows:

> When you meet your enemies in the fight, behave yourself as befits
> a good Muslim.... If [God] gives you victory, do not abuse your

advantages and beware not to stain your swords with the blood of the one who yields, neither you touch the children, the women, nor the infirm men whom you may find among your enemies. In your march through enemy territory, do not cut down the palm, or other fruit-trees, destroy not the products of the earth, ravage no fields, burn no houses....Let no destruction be made without necessity....Do not disturb the quiet of the monks and the hermits, and destroy not their abodes.

Similar orders were issued by the other three orthodox caliphs 'Umar, 'Uthmān, and 'Alī, respectively. Based on classical Islamic sources, Hamidullah has identified that acts prohibited in warfare under Islamic law include unnecessary cruel and torturous ways of killing, killing non-combatants, decapitation of prisoners of war, mutilation of humans or beasts, treachery and perfidy, devastation, destruction of harvests and unnecessary cutting of trees, excess and wickedness, adultery and fornication even with captive women, killing enemy hostages, mutilating fallen enemies, massacre, burning captured humans or animals to death, using poisonous arrows, and acts forbidden under treaties. Thus all such atrocities committed, purportedly in the name of Islam, by extremist groups such as ISIS in Iraq and Syria, Boko Haram in Nigeria, and Al-Shabab in Somalia and Kenya are not only contrary to contemporary international humanitarian law but also violate the rules of Islamic humanitarian law under *al-siyar*.

Human rights law

International human rights law compels all states to recognize, promote, and protect respect for the inherent dignity of all human beings without discrimination. Respect for human dignity is amongst established universal norms identified as '*al-ma'rūf*' under Islamic law. The basic Qur'anic provision that enjoins the protection of human dignity is Q17:70—'And We have bestowed dignity on the progeny of Adam [i.e. human beings] and elevated them on land and sea and provided them of all good things and made them to excel above most of Our creation.' This establishes the sacredness of human dignity, which the state has a duty under Islamic law to uphold. This could be either through national law or relevant treaties ratified by the state pursuant to international cooperation. The preamble of the Cairo Declaration on Human Rights in Islam adopted by the Organization of Islamic Cooperation (OIC) in 1990 declares the wish of the member Muslim-majority countries 'to contribute to the efforts of mankind to assert human rights, to protect man from exploitation and persecution, and to affirm his freedom and right to a dignified life in accordance with the Islamic *sharīʿah*'. It also states that the fundamental rights and universal freedoms are an integral part of Islam and are binding divine commandments which no one has the right to suspend, violate, or ignore. There is increasing contemporary literature aimed at establishing the concept of human rights from within Islamic classical jurisprudence and identifying a common moral ground and linkage between the general object and purpose of international human rights law and Islamic law.

The relevance of understanding the relationship between Islamic international law and contemporary international law is evidenced by the volume of increasing literature on the subject. Apart from the different aspects discussed above, there is literature covering other areas such as Islamic diplomatic law and Islamic law of the sea, amongst many others. As advocated by Shihata in 1963, a proper understanding of the rules of Islamic international law can go a long way in contributing to the development of customary international law and enhancing its acceptability in the Muslim world.

Chapter 9
Administration of justice

Islamic law recognizes the importance of adjudication (*al-qadā'*, pl. *al-aqdiyah*) for the purpose of administration of justice. Most classical *fiqh* manuals have a 'chapter on adjudication' (*kitāb al-aqdiyah*) covering the Islamic rules on administration of justice. Upholding justice is generally enjoined in Qur'anic verses such as Q4:58—'... when you judge between people, you should maintain justice...', and *ahādīth* such as: 'Judges are of three types, one will go to paradise and two to hell. The one who will go to paradise is he who knows the right and gives judgment accordingly; but he who knows the right but acts unjustly in his judgment will go to hell, and he who gives judgment based on ignorance will also go to hell' (Abū Dāwud). The divine sources mainly enjoin substantive justice while relevant details on judicial procedure were formulated jurisprudentially by the classical jurists.

Muslim jurists traced the development of Islamic administration of justice back to the Prophet's practices derived from the judicial authority conferred on him by Qur'anic provisions such as Q4:65—'... they can have no real faith until they make you [Muhammad] judge in all disputes between them, and find in their souls no resistance against your decisions, but accept them with full conviction', followed by the practices of the orthodox caliphs and rising to its peak during Abbāsid rule when the judicial processes and institutions were formally established. Western scholars such as Schacht have argued that 'the first caliphs did not appoint *qāḍīs* and in general did not lay the foundations of what later became the Islamic system of administration of justice' but that its foundation was laid during Umayyad rule. That view has been contested by Muslim scholars such as Zafar Ansari, Muhammad Guraya, and Ṭāhā Al-Alwānī, who note that the administration of justice started with the Prophet in Madīnah and was consolidated in form and procedure under the Abbāsids. Thus, the processes of administration of justice in Islamic law have never been static or inflexible but leave room for necessary refinement as the needs of substantive justice demand. Such refinements are left to the jurists and the relevant state authorities to decide in accordance with the *sharī'ah* from time to time. The jurisprudential rules relate to the appointment and role of judges, structure of courts, rules of procedure, rules of evidence, appeals and judicial reviews, etc.

Appointment and role of judges

Judgeship is a highly revered position under Islamic law, and considered as one of the roles performed by the prophets. Coulson noted that Prophet Muhammad was 'elevated to the position of judge supreme' in Madīnah, with people bringing cases to him for adjudication. He also delegated judicial authority to some of his companions such as Mu'ādh ibn Jabal and Abū Mūsā al-Ash'arī whom he appointed as judges to some of the provinces. After his death judicial authority became part of the duties of the caliphs, who also appointed judges by delegation (*istinābah*). Judges could also be appointed by any of the caliphs' governors to whom such power was delegated. Caliph 'Umar is noted as the first caliph to formally separate judicial functions from the functions of the caliph. His famous epistle to Abū Mūsā al-Ash'arī, on delegating the latter as a judge to Basrah, is considered as the foundation for formal rules on administration of justice under Islamic law. The epistle outlines the functions and responsibilities of a judge with references to ensuring equality of parties before the court, production and consideration of evidence, retraction of erroneous decisions, resort to *ijtihād*, and judicial comportment, etc.

Judgeship is legally classified as a public obligation (*fard kifāyah*), which is discharged on appointment of a qualified person to the role. A judge (*qādī*) must possess full qualifications of knowledge, character, and conduct. The classical jurists list between three and thirty conditions for a person to be eligible for appointment as a *qādī*. This belies Max Weber's derogatory notion of '*kadijustiz*' adduced by Justice Frankfurter in the case of *Terminiello v City of Chicago* [1949] in which he pejoratively pictured the *sharī'ah* court as 'a tribunal unbounded by rules' and the *qādī* as an illiterate sitting 'under a tree dispensing justice according to consideration of individual expediency'. That view is erroneous, as a *qādī* must fulfil stringent qualifications of knowledge and character for his appointment to be valid and to enable him to dispense justice in accordance with Islamic law.

In his *al-ahkām al-sultāniyyah*, al-Māwardī identifies seven basic requirements, combining knowledge and character, for appointment to the office of *qādī*. With regard to knowledge, he identifies that the *qādī* 'must have knowledge of the laws of the *sharī'ah* and his knowledge must extend to a comprehension of its principles and to the execution of legal decisions based on these principles'. The jurists differ on whether the *qādī* has to be a *mujtahid*, with the Shāfi'īs, the Shī'ahs, and Ibn Quddāmah holding that a *qādī* has to be a *mujtahid*, while the Hanafīs opine that a non-*mujtahid* could be appointed as *qādī*. Imām Mālik held that a *qādī* has to, at least, be well versed in Islamic jurisprudence (*faqīh*). Ghulam Azad argues that these different juristic views were 'correct in respect of the time and circumstances of the aforementioned scholars'. In most Muslim-majority countries today, a non-*mujtahid* may only be appointed as a *qādī* for the lower *sharī'ah* courts where *ijtihād* is not often required, while a *qādī* for the superior *sharī'ah* courts must be a qualified *mujtahid* and required to exercise *ijtihād* in necessary cases before him.

The qualification of character and conduct relates generally to piety and probity, with al-Māwardī stating that this requires a person to be, *inter alia*, righteous, just, truthful, free from forbidden acts, and equitable both when sober or angry. Notably, al-Māwardī and other classical jurists mention a contentious condition that requires attention in view of contemporary developments, namely that the *qāḍī* must be male. Ibn Rushd states in his *bidāyah al-mujtahid* that while a majority of jurists hold that being male is a required condition for the validity of judgeship, Imām Abū Ḥanīfah held that it is permissible to appoint a woman as a *qāḍī* in cases involving financial claims, while Imām Jarīr al-Ṭabarī asserted that it is permitted for a woman to be a judge in all cases without restriction. The classical majority view on this point is apparently out of date for contemporary times and most Muslim-majority countries have adopted the position of Imām al-Ṭabarī on this point. For example, in 1982, a petition was brought before the Federal Shariat Court of Pakistan in the case of *Ansar Burney v Federation of Pakistan* challenging the appointment of women judges as being violative of the *sharīʿah*. In his judgment, Justice Aftab Hussain, CJ, extensively examined the different opinions of classical Islamic jurists on the issue and, relying on the view of Imām al-Ṭabarī and a similar view attributed to Imām Mālik, found that the appointment of women judges was not contrary to the *sharīʿah*. Many Muslim-majority countries have adopted this position and appointed female judges at different judicial levels today.

Structure of courts and judicial procedure

The structure of *shariʿah* courts has evolved over time. Based on the Prophet's practice in Madīnah, the classical jurists agree that the *qāḍī* could hold court wherever is suitable but preferably in the mosque. In appointing a *qāḍī*, his terms of appointment including the scope of his functional and territorial jurisdiction must be clarified to distinguish him from other judges. The regular *qāḍī* court is normally a court of general jurisdiction that hears both civil and criminal matters. Apart from the *qāḍī* courts, the police (*shurta* or *hisbah*) courts for the control of public morality and the *mazālim* tribunal for dealing with administrative injustices were later established during Abbāsid rule. Moving forward and in response to the needs of substantive justice in contemporary times, Muslim-majority countries have today adopted different models of *sharī'ah* court structures within the permissible limits of the *shari'ah* (see Figure 8).

With regards to procedure, the first task of a *qāḍī*, at the commencement of a case, is to identify which of the parties is the claimant (*mudda'ī*) and which is the defendant (*mudda'ā alayh*). Generally, the *mudda'ī* is the party who seeks a remedy and the *mudda'ā alayh* is the party from whom remedy is sought. The judge must then decide whether the claim (*da'wah*) conforms

8. The Saudi Arabian General Court Building in Riyadh.

with relevant rules for a valid claim (*da'wah sahīhah*). The claim must disclose a cause of action and the person against whom it is brought must be specified. Also, the claim must be possible and put forward with certainty. In presenting their case, the claimant's statement is called the *maqāl* and the defendant's response is called the *jawāb*. The defendant's response could be either an admission of the claim (*iqrār*), a denial of the claim (*inkār*), or a part-admission or part-denial. A defendant's admission establishes the claim and the judge will make a decision accordingly. A defendant's denial joins the issues and the claimant would need to adduce evidence to prove his claim after which the defendant may adduce counter-evidence to contradict it. This is based on the *hadīth* that 'If people were given whatever they claimed, men would claim the wealth and blood of others; thus the burden of proof is upon the claimant and the oath is incumbent upon the denier' (al-Bayhaqī). Criminal offences must be proved beyond any iota of doubt, based on the *hadīth* that says: 'Avert the *hudūd* punishments in case of doubts.'

Rules of evidence

The main duty of a judge in any legal system is to try to establish the truth of any case before the court and the best means of doing so is through evidence, as judges are not normally privy to the events that gave rise to the case before them. Under Islamic law, evidence is known as *al-bayyinah* and the two main methods of procuring evidence are through witness testimony (*shahādah*) and defendant's confession (*iqrār*). Other alternative methods of evidence on which the jurists hold different views are circumstantial evidence (*qarā'in*), oath (*qasam*), and use of the judge's personal pre-trial knowledge (*ilm al-qādī*) about issues before the court. Ibn Rushd notes that 'A judgment may be based on (one or more) of four things: testimony, oath, refusal to take an oath and confession. It may also be based on a combination of these.'

The most important requirement regarding witnesses is credibility. Qur'anic provisions on witnesses are usually qualified by the term 'credible' (*ādil*), indicating that witnesses must be credible for their testimonies to be acceptable. There are juristic differences as to whether the credibility of a witness should be presumed or that it must be positively established for the testimony to be acceptable. A majority of the classical jurists held that the credibility of a witness must be positively established through the process of witness-vetting known as '*tazkiyyah al-shuhūd*', especially in *hudūd* cases. Conversely, the Hanafī and Zāhirī schools held that a witness's credibility should be presumed unless the contrary is proved.

Apart from the crime of *zinā*, for which Q4:15 prescribes four witnesses for proving the case, two credible witnesses are prescribed for all other crimes and transactions. The provision of Q2:282, which substitutes the testimony of one man with that of two women in a contract of debt, has been a subject of heated debate about gender discrimination in Islamic law of evidence. Although this provision has traditionally been imposed on all transactions, contemporary Muslim scholars have argued that it does not apply in all cases because apart from Q2:282 all other Qur'anic provisions on number of witnesses, such as Q4:15 and 5:106, are gender neutral and emphasize only the credibility of witnesses. Anwarullah argues that apart from *zinā* all the other Qur'anic verses on number of witnesses are not in a strict judicial sense, but relate to general day-to-day matters amongst Muslims. Witnesses can also be subpoenaed to give evidence in court and must not refuse to do so when summoned, based on Q2:282—'... and the witnesses must not refuse when they are summoned [to give evidence]'.

Similarly, there are conditions attached to confession as a means of proving crimes under Islamic law, the most important of which are that the confession must be completely voluntary and must be detailed, with the confessor being aware of the crime he is confessing to and the punishment prescribed for it. Furthermore, the confession can be withdrawn by the accused up to the point of execution of the punishment based on it.

Appeals and judicial review

Some scholars have expressed the view that there is no recognition of an appellate structure within the Islamic judicial system. This view has been challenged by different scholars such as David Powers, Hashim Kamali, and Mashood Baderin, who all argue that appeals and judicial reviews are recognized under Islamic law. Baderin highlights the fact that Abū Yūsuf was the first Chief Justice (*qāḍī al-quḍāt*) appointed by the Abbāsid caliph, Hārun al-Rashīd, in the 8th century and could hear appeals and review the decisions of other judges in the Islamic empire.

Alternative means of settling disputes

Islamic law also recognizes alternative non-judicial means of settling disputes such as arbitration or mediation (*tahkīm*) and amicable settlement or conciliation (*sulh*). For *tahkīm*, reference is often made to Q4:35—'And if you fear a breach between the two [husband and wife], then appoint an arbiter from his people and an arbiter from her people; if they both desire agreement, God will effect harmony between them.' For *sulh* the reference is to Q4:128—'And if a woman fears ill treatment or desertion on the part of her husband, there is no blame on them, if they effect a conciliation between them, and conciliation is better...'. Although both verses refer specifically to matrimonial causes, they, by analogy, apply to all other civil transactions. Both *tahkīm* and *sulh* are not allowed in criminal matters or matters involving the rights of third parties.

Contemporary reforms in juridical procedural rules

While the chapters on administration of justice in the classical *fiqh* manuals serve as starting points, they are not necessarily meant to be immutable. Many Muslim-majority countries have produced updated procedural rules for the administration of justice in their *sharī'ah* courts as is required to ensure substantive justice in today's world. The non-sacrosanct nature of judicial procedural rules under the *sharī'ah* is reflected, for example, in Saudi Arabia's enactment of a Law of Procedure before Sharī'ah Courts in 2000 containing 266 articles and a Law of Criminal Procedure in 2001 containing 225 articles. Most of the provisions in both laws would not necessarily be found in classical *fiqh* manuals but are based on procedural norms that ensure an effective administration of justice in contemporary times. There have been similar endeavours by other Muslim-majority countries, showing that there is broad flexibility within the *sharī'ah* in formulating rules of procedure for better administration of justice under Islamic law as this falls mostly within the realms of *fiqh* rather than the substantive provisions of the *sharī'ah*, per se.

Chapter 10
The future of Islamic law

After a holistic analysis of Islamic law in the preceding chapters, it is logical to round up with perceptions on the practice of Islamic law into the future. In 1959, James Anderson identified in his *Islamic Law in the Modern World* that the 'legal systems of the Muslim world may be broadly divided into three groups: (1) those that still regard the Shari'a as the fundamental law and still apply it more or less in its entirety; (2) those that have abandoned the Shari'a and have substituted a wholly secular law; and (3) those that have reached some compromise between these two positions'. He cited at the time countries such as Saudi Arabia, Northern Nigeria, Yemen, and Afghanistan as examples of the first group, Turkey as an example of the second group, and countries such as Egypt, Lebanon, Jordan, Tunisia, and Morocco as examples of the third group. The situation is much more strengthened today in most Muslim-majority countries with constitutional provisions recognizing the application of Islamic law in one form or another.

For example, Saudi Arabia asserts full application of Islamic law as state law with article 1 of the Saudi Basic Law of Governance 1992 providing that its constitution is the Qur'an and the *Sunnah*, 'which are the ultimate sources of reference' for all laws in the country. Relevant traditional mechanisms and institutions for the implementation of Islamic law are maintained but with some in a reformed mode. Article 48 of the Basic Law provides that: 'The Courts shall apply rules of the Islamic Sharia in cases that are brought before them, according to the Holy Qur'an and the Sunna, and according to laws which are decreed by the ruler in agreement with the Holy Qur'an and the Sunna', while article 46 provides that: 'The decisions of judges shall not be subject to any authority than the authority of the Islamic Sharia.' Other similar constitutional recognitions of Islamic law include: article 3 of the Constitution of Afghanistan; article 2 of the Constitution of Egypt; articles 4 and 12 of the Constitution of Iran; article 2 of the Constitution of Iraq; the 9th schedule of the Constitution of Malaysia; article 10 of the Constitution of Maldives; articles 260, 262, and 275 of the Constitution of Nigeria; and article 227 of the Constitution of Pakistan.

There are also applicable statutes in the form of penal codes, personal status laws, and family codes based on Islamic law in different Muslim-majority countries today. Classical *fiqh* continues to apply in different Muslim jurisdictions, with Hanafi jurisprudence currently dominant in countries such as Jordan, Pakistan, Afghanistan, and Turkey; Shāfiʿī jurisprudence dominant in countries such as Indonesia, Malaysia, Somalia, Djibouti, and Maldives, Mālikī jurisprudence dominant in countries such as Nigeria, Mauritania, and Bahrain; and Hanbalī jurisprudence dominant in countries such as Saudi Arabia and Qatar. Islamic personal status law is also applied today in some secular Muslim-minority countries such as Kenya, the Philippines, and Thailand, where there are *qādī* courts for its application amongst the Muslim minorities.

Owing to the influence of modern state structures and modern modes of law-making, the form and application of Islamic law as part of state law today is not based strictly on direct reference to classical *fiqh* manuals, but indirectly through state legislation in the form of codified statutes. Rudolph Peters has observed in that regard that:

As a result of the process of codification that has continued for nearly a century and a half, there are hardly any countries left where the shari'a is applied without codification....This means that nearly everywhere the state has assumed the power to determine what the shari'a norms are, at least in those fields that are enforced as part of the national legal system....This [has] led some, mainly Western, non-Muslim scholars to question whether this legislation can still be regarded as shari'a and as Islamic. Raising this question is...not very relevant and betrays a certain polemical point of view. By arguing that codified shari'a is not shari'a and not Islamic anymore, they want to demonstrate that the re-Islamization of the law that was introduced in some countries was not real re-introduction of the shari'a.

This is perceived as a transformation of Islamic law or the *sharī'ah* from jurists' law to statute law and a displacement of traditional *ulamā'* as sole interpreters of the *sharī'ah*, triggering theoretical debates about whether such statutes can still be considered as 'Islamic law'. In engaging with that debate Aharon Layish highlights Hallaq's view that 'traditional shari'a can surely be said to have gone without return'. That view is very far-fetched if the term *sharī'ah* is restricted to the Qur'an and *Sunnah*, as both, in contrast to *fiqh*, have remained intact as fundamental material sources for Islamic law up till today and understandably into the future. But if the view is confined to *fiqh* or Islamic law in practice, then it raises two questions with regard to the future of Islamic law, one relating to form and the other to content.

In relation to form, the question is whether codification deprives Islamic law of its status of being 'Islamic'. A strictly historical perspective that tends to restrict Islamic law to the past may argue that it does, while an evolutionary perspective would see codification as part of the evolution of Islamic law. Codification ensures certainty of the law and is reflected in the compilation of basic legal codes such as *kitāb al-kharrāj*, an Islamic revenue code written by Imām Abū Yūsuf at the request of Caliph Harūn Rashīd during the classical period of Islamic law in the 8th century. Also, restricting the *ulamā'* who are entitled to interpret the *sharī'ah* to the so-called 'traditional *ulamā'* is a very reductive use of the term *ulamā'*.

In relation to content, it is noteworthy that most modern Islamic law statutes are often based on classical *fiqh* of a particular jurisprudential school or a mixture of rulings from different jurisprudential schools using the principles of *takhayyur* and/or *talfīq*. The statutes also often refer to the concept of *ijtihād* to justify any reforms that are made to classical *fiqh* on particular issues. For example, the preamble of the Moroccan Family Code 2004 indicates that the code was prepared by 'an advisory Royal Commission constituted of the finest experts and religious scholars' who were advised by the King to rely on 'the provisions of *Sharia*...and encouraged the use of *ijtihād* to deduce laws and precepts, while taking into consideration the spirit of our modern era'. Thus, the contents of most modern Islamic law statutes often substantively reproduce classical Islamic jurisprudence. Anderson highlighted this by reference to the modern codification of Islamic law under the Tanzīmāt reforms during the Ottoman Empire in the 19th century, arguing that the codes were 'on the basis of precepts derived not from European law but from the Sharī'a [and that] the Majalla represents the earliest example of the reduction of Islamic law to the form of modern legislative enactment'.

One aspect of classical *fiqh* that may be affected by codified Islamic law is the flexibility of *ikhtilāf* (differences of juristic opinion), as the codified *fiqh* becomes the applicable law. However, the classical Islamic legal maxim *'hukm al-hākim yarfa' al-khilāf'* ('the ruling authority's edict resolves jurisprudential differences') could be relied upon to justify such codification. Peters has argued credibly that in addressing the question of whether or not codified Islamic law statutes can still be considered as 'Islamic' the 'only correct answer would be that if Muslims hold that it is Islamic and a legitimate...interpretation of the shari'a, which most Muslims do, there are no good arguments to view it differently'.

While the future of Islamic law in the Muslim world continues to attract academic debates, it is evident that Islamic law must continue to evolve into the foreseeable future in response to the dynamics of human society within the flexible limits of the *sharī'ah*. Certainly, the Qur'an and the *Sunnah* will continue to serve as the fundamental divine sources, and classical *fiqh* will continue to serve as reference for statutory codifications, especially in the areas of family and personal status laws in most Muslim-majority countries. The rules of classical Islamic legal theory (*usūl al-fiqh*) will also continue to be relevant in the jurisprudential debates regarding reforms to classical jurisprudential views into the foreseeable future.

References

Chapter 1: Historical development

'Muhammad had perceived...': Amstrong, K. (2001) *Islam: A Short History*, London: Phoenix Press, pp. 4–5.

'betrays a highly legalistic...': Goitien, S. D. (1960) 'The Birth-Hour of Muslim Law?: An Essay in Exegesis', 50 *Muslim World*, pp. 23–9, at p. 25.

'light on the Prophet's capacity...': Ansari, Z. (1992) 'The Contribution of the Qur'an and the Prophet to the Development of Islamic Fiqh', 3 *Journal of Islamic Studies*, No. 2, pp. 141–71, at p. 146.

'already in the first/seventh century...': Motzki, H. (2002) *The Origins of Islamic Jurisprudence: Meccan Fiqh Before the Classical Schools*, Leiden: Brill, p. 295.

'must have had a primary legal...': Hallaq, W. (1999) *A History of Islamic Legal Theories: An Introduction to Sunnī Usūl al-Fiqh*, Cambridge: Cambridge University Press, p. 8.

'was originally created...': Ibn Khaldūn (1377) *The Muqadimmah: An Introduction to History*, translated by Franz Rosenthal 1967, Princeton: Princeton University Press, p. 207.

'for greater unity, coherence and...': Arabi, O. (2001) *Studies in Modern Islamic Law and Jurisprudence*, The Hague: Kluwer Law International, p. 21.

Chapter 2: The nature of Islamic law

'Although Islamic law is a "sacred law"...': Schacht, J. (1946) *An Introduction to Islamic Law*, Oxford: The Clarendon Press, p. 4.

'whatever the state enforces...': An-Na'im, A. A. (2013) 'Towards an
   Islamic Society, not an Islamic State' in Griffith-Jones, R. (ed.)
   Islam and English Law, Cambridge: Cambridge University Press,
   pp. 238–44 at pp. 239–40.
'is confined to law properly...': Coulson, N. J. (1964) *A History of
   Islamic Law*, Edinburgh: Edinburgh University Press, p. 84.
'This law satisfies the criteria...': Twinning, W. (2009) *General
   Jurisprudence: Understanding Law from Global Perspectives*,
   Cambridge: Cambridge University Press, p. 89.
'though God has given us a revelation...': Qadri, A. A. (1986) *Islamic
   Jurisprudence in the Modern World*, Delhi: Taj Company, p. 199.
'confusion arises when the term...': 'Abd al 'Atī, H. (1977) *The Family
   Structure in Islam*, Indianapolis: American Trust
   Publications, p. 14.

Chapter 3: Theory, scope, and practice

'not in the introduction of...': Coulson, N. J. (1964) *A History of
   Islamic Law*, Edinburgh: Edinburgh University Press, p. 55.
'[n]o more than approximately eighty...': ibid. p. 12.
'[t]here are close to 350 legal...': Kamali, M. H. (2003) *Principles of
   Islamic Jurisprudence*, 3rd edn, Cambridge: Islamic Texts
   Society, p. 26.
'extra-Quranic law-making capacity': Coulson, N. J. (1964)
   above, p. 22.
'they all share one fundamental...': Hallaq, W. (1999) 'The
   Authenticity of Prophetic Hadith: A Pseudo-problem', 89 *Studia
   Islamica*, pp. 75–90 at pp. 76–7.
'In the Qur'an and *Sunnah*, Muslims believe...': Nadwi, M. A. (2007)
   Al-Muhaddithāt: The Women Scholars in Islam, Oxford: Interface
   Publications Ltd, p. 2.
'[w]hat was the constituting group...': Hourani, G. F. (1964) 'The
   Basis of Authority of Consensus in Sunnite Islam', 21 *Studia
   Islamica*, pp. 13–60 at p. 17.
'the fact that substantive law embodied...': Hallaq, W. B. (1994)
   'From *Fatwās* to *Furū'*: Growth and Change in Islamic
   Substantive Law', 1 *Islamic Law and Society*, No. 1, pp. 29–65
   at pp. 30–1.

Chapter 4: Family law

'not accurate, therefore, to designate…': 'Abd al 'Aṭī, H. (1977) *The Family Structure in Islam*, Plainfield: American Trust Publications, p. 59.

'The volume of maintenance claims…': Welchman, L., (2007) *Women and Muslim Family Laws in Arab States*, Amsterdam: Amsterdam University Press, p. 93.

'If separation occurs between…': Nyazee, I. A. K. (trans.) (2008) *Al-Hidāyah: The Guidance, Burhān al-Dīn al-Farghānī al-Marghīnānī*, Vol. 2, Bristol: Amal Press, p. 79.

'It is a well-established principle that…': Zin, N. M. (2003) 'For the Best Interest of the Child: The Impact of the New Approach of Custody Order in Malaysian Legislation', 11 *IIUM Law Journal*, No. 1, pp. 63–81 at p. 64.

'the protection of the interests of…': Zahraa, M., and Malek, N. A. (1998) 'The Concept of Custody in Islamic Law', 13 *Arab Law Quarterly*, No. 2, pp. 155–77 at p. 159.

'ensure that civil marriages are…': Independent Review into the application of sharia law in England and Wales Presented to Parliament by the Secretary of State for the Home Department by Command of Her Majesty (2018), p. 17.

Chapter 5: Law of inheritance

'[t]here is no part of…': Anderson, J. N. D. (1965) 'Recent Reforms in the Islamic Law of Inheritance', 14 *The International Comparative Law Quarterly*, No. 2, pp. 349–465 at p. 349.

'when the provisions regarding…': ibid.

'comprises, beyond question…': Rumsey, A. (1880) *Moohummudan Law of Inheritance and Rights of Relations Affecting it: Sunni Doctine*, London: W. H. Allen & Co. p. iii.

'it is inaccurate, at the very least,…': Chaudhry, Z. (1998) 'The Myth of Misogyny: A Reanalysis of Women's Inheritance in Islamic Law', 61 *Albany Law Review*, pp. 511–55 at p. 537.

'Islamic inheritance law does not…': Christmann, A. (trans.) (2009) *The Qur'an, Morality and Critical Reason: The Essential Muhammad Sharur*, Leiden: Brill, p. 206.

Chapter 6: Law of financial transactions

'emerged as one of the most…': Vogel, F. E., and Hayes, S. L. (2006) *Islamic Law and Finance: Religion, Risk and Return*, Leiden: Brill, p. 2.

'any increase charged in a loan…': Saeed, A. (1999) *Islamic Banking and Interest: A Study of the Prohibion of Riba and its Contemporary Interpretation*, Leiden: Brill, p. 17.

'the exploitation of the economically…': ibid.

'interest on certain interest-based…': Vogel, F. E., and Hayes, S. L., (2006) above, p. 46.

'[s]ome people in our modern times…': Salahi, A., and Shamis, A., (trans.) (2000) *Sayyid Qutb, In the Shade of the Qur'an*, Vol. 2, Leicester: The Islamic Foundation, p. 211.

'the sale of probable items…': El-Gamal, M. A. (2011) *Islamic Finance: Law, Economics and Practice*, Cambridge: Cambridge University Press, p. 58.

'Islamic finance is thriving in Europe…': Wilson, R. (2007) *Islamic Finance in Europe* RSCAS Policy Papers No. 2007/02, Italy: European University Institute, p. 1.

Chapter 7: Penal law

'taking the property of another…': Nyazee, I. A. K. (trans.) (2000) *The Distinguished Jurist's Primer: Bidāyat al-Mujtahid wa Nihāyat al-Muqtasid*, Vol. 2, Reading: Garnet Publishing Ltd, p. 536.

'waiting by the way (or highway)…': El-Awa, M. S. (1984) *Punishment in Islamic Law*, Indianapolis: American Trust Publications, p. 8.

'all sexual intercourse between…': ibid. p. 4.

'[M]uslim jurists are in agreement to the effect…': Kamali, M. H. (2019) *Crime and Punishment in Islamic Law: A Fresh Interpretation*, Oxford: OUP, p. 67.

'unproved allegation that…': El-Awa, M. S. (1984) above, p. 20.

'[t]he basis of Muslim polity…': Hamidullah, M. (1997) *The Muslim Conduct of State*, revised 7th edn, Lahore: Sh Muhammad Ashraf, p. 174.

'have a dual nature, that of…': El-Awa, M. S. (1984) above, p. 85.

'Muslim countries and jurisdictions…': Kamali, M. H. (2019) *Crime and Punishment in Islamic Law: A Fresh Interpretation*, Oxford: OUP, p. 2.

Chapter 8: International law (*al-siyar*)

'to verify the extent of…': Shihata, I. (1962) 'Islamic Law and the
World Community', 4 *Harvard International Club Journal*,
pp. 101–13 at pp. 101–2.

'[w]hen jihād is invoked by…': Mahmoudi, S. (2005) 'The Islamic
Perception of the Use of Force in the Contemporary World', 7
Journal of the History of International Law, pp. 55–68 at p. 67.

'the ethics of humanitarian…': Hashmi, S. H. (2003) 'Is There an
Islamic Ethic of Humanitarian Intervention?' in Lang, A. F., Jr
(ed.) *Just Intervention*, Washington, DC: Georgetown University
Press, pp. 62–83 at p. 69.

'codified in the eighth century…': Bassiouni, M. C. (2014) *The Shari'a
and Islamic Criminal Justice in Time of War and Peace*,
Cambridge: Cambridge University Press, p. 162.

'…never commit breach of trust…': Bennoune, K. (1994) 'Assalāmu
Alaykum?: Humanitarian Law in Islamic Jurisprudence', 15
Michigan Journal of International Law, pp. 605–43 at p. 624.

'When you meet your enemies…': ibid. p. 626.

Chapter 9: Administration of justice

'the first caliphs did not…': Schacht, J. (1955) 'Pre-Islamic Background
and Early Development of Jurisprudence' in Khadduri, M., and
Liebesney, H. (eds) *Law in the Middle East*, Vol. 1, Washington,
DC: The Middle East Institute, pp. 29–56 at p. 34.

'elevated to the position of…': Coulson, N. J. (1964) *A History of
Islamic Law*, Edinburgh: Edinburgh University Press, p. 22.

'must have knowledge of…': Yate, A. (trans.) (1996) *al-Ahkām
as-Sultāniyyah: The Laws of Islamic Governance, Abu'l Hasan
al-Mawardi*, London: Ta Ha Publishers, p. 100.

'correct in respect of the…': Azad, G. M. (1987) *Judicial System of
Islam*, Islamabad: Islamic Research Institute, p. 21.

'A judgement may be based on…': Nyazee, I. A. K. (trans.) (2000) *The
Distinguished Jurist's Primer: Bidāyatal-Mujtahid wa Nihāyat
al-Muqtasid*, Vol. 2, Reading: Garnet Publishing Ltd, p. 556.

Chapter 10: The future of Islamic law

'legal systems of the Muslim world…': Anderson, J. N. D. (1959) *Islamic
Law in the Muslim World*, London: Stevens & Sons, pp. 82–3.

'As a result of the process of codification…': Peters, R. (2002) 'From Jurists' Law to Statute Law or What Happens When the Shari'a is Codified?', 7 *Mediterranian Politics*, pp. 82–95 at pp. 92–3.

'traditional shari'a can surely…': Layish, A. (2014) 'Islamic Law in the Modern World: Nationalization, Islamization, Reinstatement', 21 *Islamic Law and Society*, pp. 276–307 at p. 277.

'on the basis of precepts derived…': Anderson, J. N. D. (1960) 'The Significance of Islamic Law in the World Today', 9 *The American Journal of Comparative Law*, No. 2, pp. 187–98 at pp. 188–9.

'only correct answer would be…': Peters, R. (2002) 'From Jurists' Law to Statute Law or What Happens when the Shari'a is Codified', 7 *Mediterranean Politics*, pp. 82–95 at p. 93.

Further reading

Chapter 1: Historical development

Al-Azami, M. M. (1996) *On Schacht's Origins of Muhammadan Jurisprudence*, Oxford: OCIS.

Coulson, N. J. (1964) *A History of Islamic Law*, Edinburgh: Edinburgh University Press.

Faruqi, M. Y. (2007) *Development of Usul al-Fiqh: An Early Historical Perspective*, New Delhi: Adam Publishers & Distributors.

Schacht, J. (1950) *The Origins of Muhammadan Jurisprudence*, Oxford: The Clarendon Press.

Chapter 2: The nature of Islamic law

Baderin, M. A. (2009) 'Islamic Legal Theory in Context' in Baderin, M.A. (ed.) *Islamic Legal Theory*, Vol. 1, Aldershot: Ashgate Publishing, pp. xi–xxxvii.

Dupret, B. (2018) *What is the Shari'a?* London: C. Hurst & Co. (Publishers) Ltd.

Hallaq, W. B. (1997) *A History of Islamic Legal Theories*, Cambridge: Cambridge University Press.

Schacht, J. (1964) *An Introduction to Islamic Law*, Oxford: The Clarendon Press.

Chapter 3: Theory, scope, and practice

Kamali, M. H. (2003) *Principles of Islamic Jurisprudence*, 3rd edn, Cambridge: Islamic Texts Society.

Khadduri, M. (1987) *al-Shāfiʿī's Risāla: Treatise on the Foundations of Islamic Jurisprudence*, Cambridge: Islamic Texts Society.

Nyazee, I. A. (2016) *Outlines of Islamic Jurisprudence*, 6th edn, Islamabad: Centre for Excellence in Research.

Qadri, A. A. (1986) *Islamic Jurisprudence in the Modern World*, Delhi: Taj Company.

Chapter 4: Family law

ʿAbd al ʿAṭī, H. (1977) *The Family Structure in Islam*, Indianapolis: American Trust Publications.

Mansoori, M. T. (2012) *Family Law in Islam: Theory and Application*, Islamabad: Shariah Academy, International Islamic University.

Nasir, J. J. (2009) *The Islamic Law of Personal Status*, 3rd revised and updated edn, Leiden: Brill.

Welchman, L. (2014) *Women and Muslim Family Laws in Arab States: A Comparative Overview of Textual Development and Advocacy*, Amsterdam: Amsterdam University Press.

Chapter 5: Law of inheritance

Coulson, N. J. (1971) *Succession in Muslim Family Law*, Cambridge: Cambridge University Press.

Hussain, A. (2005) *The Islamic Law of Succession*, Riyadh: Maktaba Darussalam.

Khan, H. (2007) *The Islamic Law of Inheritance*, Oxford: Oxford University Press.

Chapter 6: Law of financial transactions

Aldohi, A. K. (2011) *The Legal and Regulatory Aspects of Islamic Banking: A Comparative Look at the United Kingdom and Malaysia*, London: Routledge.

Mansuri, M. T. (2006) *Islamic Law of Contracts and Business Transactions*, New Delhi: Adam Publishers and Distributors.

Usmani, M. T. (2010) *An Introduction to Islamic Finance*, Karachi: Quranic Studies Publishers.

Visser, H. (2009) *Islamic Finance: Principles and Practice*, Cheltenham: Edward Elgar.

Chapter 7: Penal law

Baderin, M. A. (2006) 'Effective Legal Representation in "Sharī'ah" Courts as a Means of Addressing Human Rights Concerns in the Islamic Criminal Justice System of Muslim States', 11 *Yearbook of Islamic and Middle Eastern Law*, 2004–2005, pp. 135–67.

Bassiouni, M. C. (ed.) (1982) *The Islamic Criminal Justice System*, New York: Oceania Publications.

Kamali, M. H. (2019) *Crime and Punishment in Islamic Law: A Fresh Interpretation*, Oxford: Oxford University Press.

Peters, R. (2006) *Crime and Punishment in Islamic Law*, Cambridge: Cambridge University Press.

Chapter 8: International law (*al-siyar*)

Baderin, M. A. (2003) *International Human Rights and Islamic Law*, Oxford: OUP.

Bsoul, L. B. (2008) *International Treaties (Mu'āhadāt) in Islam: Theory and Practice in the Light of Islamic International Law (Siyar) According to Orthodox Schools*, Lanham, MD: University Press of America.

Hamidullah, M. (1977) *The Muslim Conduct of State*, 7th edn, Lahore: Muhammad Ashraf Publishers.

Khadduri, M. (1966) *The Islamic Law of Nations: Shaybani's Siyar*, Baltimore: Johns Hopkins Press.

Chapter 9: Administration of justice

Al-Alwani, T. J. (1995) 'The Rights of the Accused in Islam', 10 *Arab Law Quarterly*, No. 4, pp. 3–16.

Anderson, J. N. D. (1949) 'Muslim Procedure and Evidence', 1 *Journal of African Administration*, pp. 123–9, 176–83.

Anwarullah (1999) *Principles of Evidence in Islam*, Kuala Lumpur: A. S. Noordeen.

Azad, G. M. (1987) *Judicial System of Islam*, Islamabad: Islamic Research Institute.

Chapter 10: The future of Islamic law

Abou El Fadl, K. (2005) *The Great Theft: Wrestling Islam from the Extremists*, New York: HarperCollins Publishers.

Ali, S. S. (2016) *Modern Challenges to Islamic Law*, Cambridge: Cambridge University Press.

Black, A., Esmaeili, H., and Hosen, N. (2013) *Modern Perspectives on Islamic Law*, Cheltenham: Edward Elgar Publishing Ltd.

Hallaq, W. B. (2014) *The Impossible State: Islam, Politics, and Modernity's Moral Predicament*, Columbia: Columbia University Press.

Otto, J. M. (ed.) (2010) *Sharia Incorporated: A Comparative Overview of the Legal Systems of Twelve Muslim Countries in Past and Present*, Leiden: Leiden University Press.

Index

For the benefit of digital users, indexed terms that span two pages (e.g., 52–53) may, on occasion, appear on only one of those pages.

N

O

P

ISLAMIC HISTORY
A Very Short Introduction
Adam J. Silverstein

Does history matter? This book argues not that history matters, but that Islamic history does. This *Very Short Introduction* introduces the story of Islamic history; the controversies surrounding its study; and the significance that it holds - for Muslims and for non-Muslims alike. Opening with a lucid overview of the rise and spread of Islam, from the seventh to twenty first century, the book charts the evolution of what was originally a small, localised community of believers into an international religion with over a billion adherents. Chapters are also dedicated to the peoples - Arabs, Persians, and Turks - who shaped Islamic history, and to three representative institutions - the mosque, jihad, and the caliphate - that highlight Islam's diversity over time.

'The book is extremely lucid, readable, sensibly organised, and wears its considerable learning, as they say, 'lightly'.'

BBC History Magazine

www.oup.com/vsi